Log Cabin Classics

Log Cabin Classics

Robbin Obomsawin

Gibbs Smith, Publisher
Salt Lake City

07 06 05 04   5 4 3 2

Published by
Gibbs Smith, Publisher
P.O. Box 667
Layton, Utah 84041

Orders: [1-800] 748-5439
www.gibbs-smith.com

Edited by Suzanne Gibbs Taylor and Jennifer Grillone
Designed by Steven Rachwal Design
Printed and bound in Hong Kong

Library of Congress Cataloging-in-Publication Data

Obomsawin, Robbin, 1960-
  Log cabin classics / Robbin Obomsawin.—1st ed.
      p. cm.
  ISBN 1-58685-315-5
  1. Log cabins—Designs and plans. 2. Architecture, Domestic—Designs
and plans. I. Title.
NA8470.O255 2003
728.7'3—dc21
                           2003007503

Contents

Acknowledgments

THIS BOOK IS DEDICATED TO the new and upcoming handcrafted log builders who will build the "cabins" of our future. Your youth and passion for the art of building log structures will transcend all other styles and trends. I hope these classic log cabins will give you the information and details you need that I did not have access to when my husband and I started log building.

There is much talent, enthusiasm, and drive in the new generation of log builders. I truly wish you the best in your ongoing journey as you recapture the romance and pioneer spirit of building a log cabin. As handcrafted log builders, we know and appreciate the hard work and stamina this form of building requires. I hope that the construction plans in this book will give you the tools you need to focus on your talents as woodcrafters and artisans. I also hope that each specially selected home will create many memories for you, and your family, friends, and clients for generations to come.

I am also grateful to all the past generations of log crafters that left us so many treasured log cabins, which have housed the pioneers of our young nation who helped form our great country. Although we may not know your names and can no longer fully appreciate the trials you experienced, the jewels you created continue to inspire us.

The magic formula to a successful building project does not happen without its elves and wizards in the background—the designers, draftspeople, architects, engineers, contractors, sub-trades, and log builder's assistants who make a finished project appear effortless. My elves are Jennifer Stalnaker and Tony Woods. These skilled artists are so often overlooked for their hard work and talent. I truly appreciate all those who have gone out of their way to ensure that our clients have achieved their dreams of the perfect log cabin, as it can be a very trying time for all involved. These are very caring people who treat their job with passion in whatever they encounter, and for that I am exceedingly grateful.

A special thanks to my editor, Suzanne Taylor, and my publisher, Gibbs Smith, who were the first to believe in my not so "small" ideas about log building. Thank you for your support and guidance, which has made it possible to share with so many the art of handcrafted log building in print. It takes a great team to create such beautiful quality books; with editing, layout, and design they seem to magically transform a pile of words and drawings into a meaningful presentation.

Another special thanks to both of my sisters-in-law, Liz Obomsawin and Marion Dickerman; my son Jim Obomsawin; and to my parents, Jim and Esther Whitman, who are always willing to help me with the many endless rounds of writing needed to build a book. I know that it seems to take so many to keep me under control, but with a creative mind comes some wild and crazy ideas!

Introduction

A log cabin is the essence of a much slower-paced and more simple way of life. The whole lifestyle of log cabin living embodies an air of romance. The intention of this book is to provide you with straightforward, creative design; practical construction advice; and timesaving and cost-saving ideas in order to give you a clear and focused point of direction. By following these suggestions and building with indigenous materials so that the home fits naturally into its surroundings, you can create a log cabin where you feel that you are always on vacation.

Log cabin architecture has an enduring impact that still influences architecture today. There is something special about a handcrafted log cabin. Perhaps it is reflective of our childhood memories when we built a lean-to or a playhouse out of wood. Whatever the reason, log cabins leave us with a magical feeling, and log building is dreamed of by the romantic soul where the warmth and beauty of wood are forms of nature that are timeless and unsurpassed.

Log Cabin Classics represents my years of experience, study, travel, and designing floor plans that are the most significant in form, function, and flow. The enclosed log cabins are homes that are from my heart and life experiences. With these designs, I strive to capture the spirit of a log cabin built with simplicity and modern conveniences.

This style of log cabin architecture is for the client who wants added thought and detail integrated into a cabin built with a respect for

This is the stuff that dreams are made of! The couple who owns this cabin is living the life so many only dream of. The log shell is only 14' x 18' with a conventionally built addition that houses the kitchen. The firewood is always stacked as though it is treated as artwork. The bedroom and bath are tucked under the house to make use of the limited space.

nature. These log cabins require the extra attention needed to elevate a structure to a higher level of character. *Log Cabin Classics* is the perfect book for new log builders who wish to build a log cabin on their own without being overwhelmed or intimidated by a large structure, and who understand that quality is more important than quantity.

A more traditional log cabin may also appeal to the first-time homeowner, empty nesters who require less space, the conservative family that values the wealth of nature, the vacation homeowner in need of simplicity, or the retired couple who wants to downsize their home so it does not consume their valuable time.

Handcrafted log cabins are a respite from mass production and are as diverse as the people who own them. We now embark on a new frontier of log building where you not only use your hands, but also your heart. Log cabin life is not just a décor, but a way of life where all is considered. Our present-day challenge is to capture this piece of romance in the modern-day home. These cabins are designed as log *castles* under 1,500 square feet, where simplicity is revered over opulence.

Log Cabin Classics concentrates on a more traditional cabin-size footprint. Some of the cabins' living spaces are extended by maximizing the use of the basement. There is a lot of living that can be had within a smaller size footprint.

It is my wish that this book of log cabin information and photography becomes a rewarding journey that will touch your heart and soul. It is also my hope that *Log Cabin Classics* will inspire you and spark your imagination so you may create a home that portrays your love of cabin life—a home that will become your own legacy for new generations to enjoy.

—Robbin Obomsawin

Lake Placid Lodge supports and features the work of many local Adirondack artisans throughout its lodge and cabin rentals. This game table is made out of antlers, birch bark, and tree saplings where manmade and nature merge into one.

Cabin Fever

 We often romanticize about the small cabin in the woods, by the lake, or atop a mountain—the home that is in tune with nature. We sometimes need to feel worlds away from the "civilization" that bogs us down with financial worry and our material possessions. If you have ever had the opportunity to stay in a small cabin, you may have felt the emotional connection to nature that echoes the spirit of cabin life. This simple home allows one to enjoy the simple, tranquil beauty of nature that is so free and rejuvenating.

Some of the most rewarding and creative projects are the homes in which there are limitations of size, footprint, or budget. When we limit ourselves to a home's overall size, it can become a freedom in that we no longer have to be tied down by extra gadgetry, added maintenance, clutter, or any of the other trappings a larger scale home can bring.

The comedic philosopher George Carlin was right on target for most of us when he defined home as "only a place to put your stuff while you go out to buy more stuff." This humor is something we can all relate to at some point in our lives.

Many people who build a log cabin as a second home enjoy the freedom of living in a much smaller space so much that they decide to sell their larger home to live full time in their cabin. They pare down their belongings to accommodate living in a much smaller space and have expressed to me how much they enjoy their newfound freedom.

A small log cabin can capture big views. A cabin does not have to be large to make those who enter feel at home.

It is not about how big or expensive a home is, but how comfortable and welcoming it feels. This warm, uncomplicated atmosphere extends beyond the four walls of a home, as we become enraptured in nature's serenity that surrounds a log cabin. The most dramatic statement of simplicity is when simplicity itself is the best accessory. Creativity can be developed with surprisingly very little—it is often sheer determination and imagination that lead the dream of building a log cabin.

There is little in life that can compare to finally realizing a long-desired dream. When that includes building your own log cabin, the thrill and emotion you will feel when you step into your finished log cabin is one you will never forget. It is a feeling that the structure is permanent, which is felt by everyone who enters; the atmosphere also offers a welcoming peace and tranquility. Your own little log cabin is a place to relax and put your feet up. The plans that follow offer a simpler form of architecture that can give you the added time to dream—and execute—bigger dreams.

ABOVE: An interior designer was used to achieve balance and texture throughout this cabin, which utilizes primarily neutral colors.

OPPOSITE: Texture is used to create warmth and depth in this cabin. Other forms of gnarled, weathered, and grey wood are scribed together to form the fireplace mantel. A free-form piece of wood was used as a light fixture.

OPPOSITE: *Dovetail joinery is artistically fitted in each corner of the structure that interlocks the connecting walls to one another. The lines may appear to be simple, but years of work are needed to accomplish this level of joinery. Note how a large, untamed knot or imperfection is used effectively within the log wall.*

LEFT: *The use of colored cabinets like these from Crown Point Cabinetry brings warm colors into a log home.*

Well-drawn cross sections tell the story of where the laying of log work fits into the structure and describes what heights and types of connections are needed. Cross sections are crucial to log home and timber-frame construction. Major problems and interesting design details can be solved with accurate drawings.

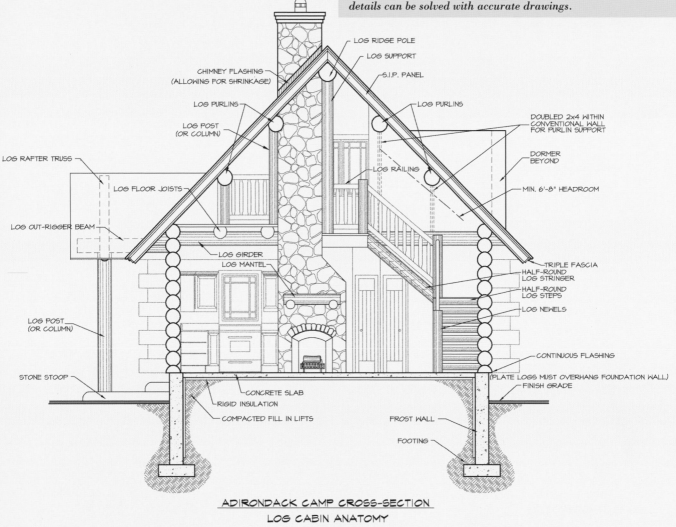

LOG RIDGE POLE

LOG SUPPORT

S.I.P. PANEL

CHIMNEY FLASHING
(ALLOWING FOR SHRINKAGE)

LOG PURLINS

LOG PURLINS

DOUBLED 2x4 WITHIN
CONVENTIONAL WALL
FOR PURLIN SUPPORT

LOG POST
(OR COLUMN)

DORMER
BEYOND

LOG RAFTER TRUSS

LOG RAILING

MIN. 6'-8" HEADROOM

LOG FLOOR JOISTS

LOG OUT-RIGGER BEAM

LOG GIRDER

LOG MANTEL

TRIPLE FASCIA

HALF-ROUND
LOG STRINGER

HALF-ROUND
LOG STEPS

LOG NEWELS

LOG POST
(OR COLUMN)

CONTINUOUS FLASHING

STONE STOOP

(PLATE LOGS MUST OVERHANG FOUNDATION WALL)

FINISH GRADE

CONCRETE SLAB

RIGID INSULATION

COMPACTED FILL IN LIFTS

FROST WALL

FOOTING

ADIRONDACK CAMP CROSS-SECTION
LOG CABIN ANATOMY

Adirondack Camp

This simple structure is the essence of log cabin living. Clean lines and classic style are any cabin's best features. This cabin has all the necessities of life with a good size kitchen, large living area, and a bunkroom and bath tucked in under the slope of the stairs. The second floor bedroom loft is artfully arranged behind the chimney's stack with the added beauty of log railings that define the loft's boundaries.

BEDROOMS: 2	
BATHS: 1	
DECKS AND PORCHES: 175 square feet	
BASEMENT: on slab	
LIVING AREA: 854 square feet	

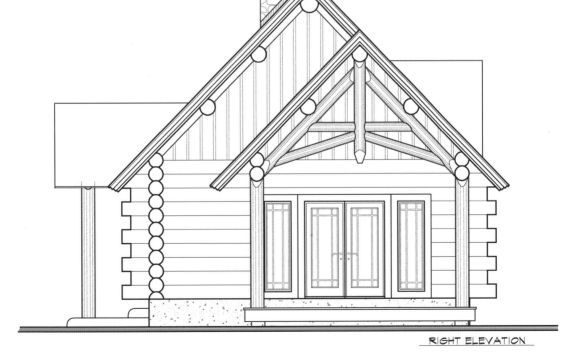

RIGHT ELEVATION

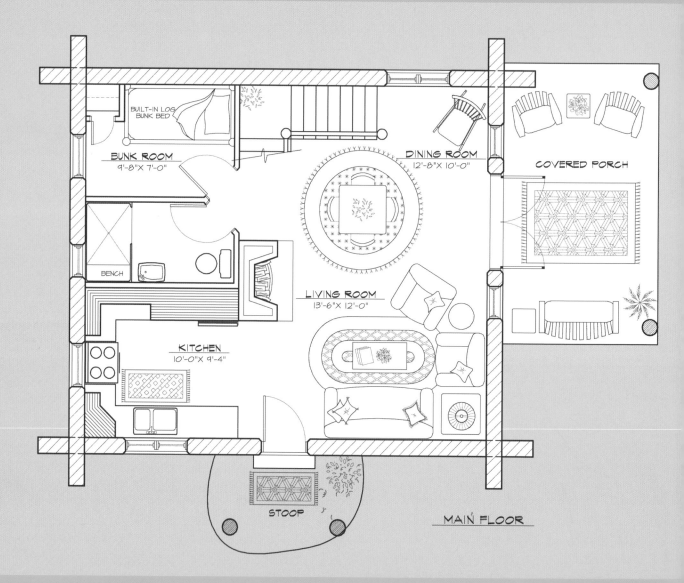

BUNK ROOM
9'-8"X 7'-0"

BUILT-IN LOG
BUNK BED

DINING ROOM
12'-8"X 10'-0"

COVERED PORCH

BENCH

LIVING ROOM
13'-6"X 12'-0"

KITCHEN
10'-0"X 9'-4"

STOOP

MAIN FLOOR

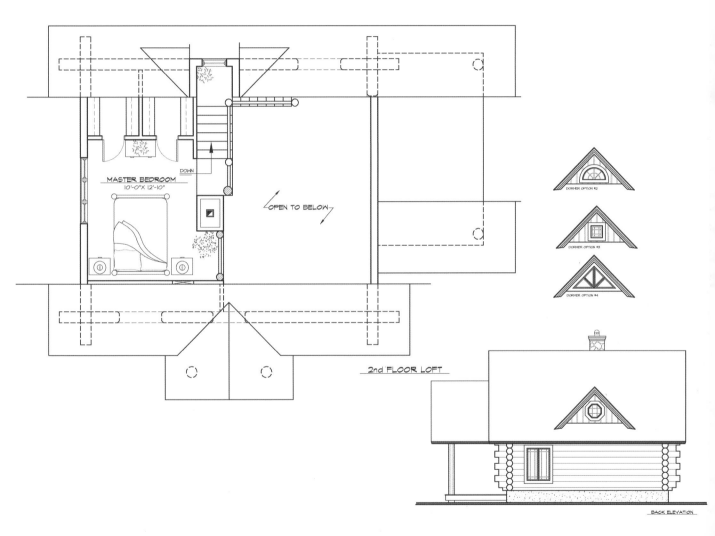

MASTER BEDROOM
10'-0" X 12'-10"

DOWN

OPEN TO BELOW

DORMER OPTION #2

DORMER OPTION #3

DORMER OPTION #4

2nd FLOOR LOFT

BACK ELEVATION

Blue Herring Bay

BEDROOMS: 2

BATHS: 1

DECKS AND PORCHES: 260 square feet

BASEMENT: 832 square feet walkout

LIVING AREA: 1,106 square feet

This log cabin has clean, classic lines with a semi-open floor plan. The entry porch uses scissors-style trusses to add architectural interest and curb appeal.

The wraparound kitchen with tucked-in refrigerator makes efficient use of this home's limited footprint. The upstairs bedroom loft is perched like an eagle's nest high above the trees. The walkout basement can be used as shown, or made into a two-bedroom retreat with recreational room. It could also be used as an in-law apartment.

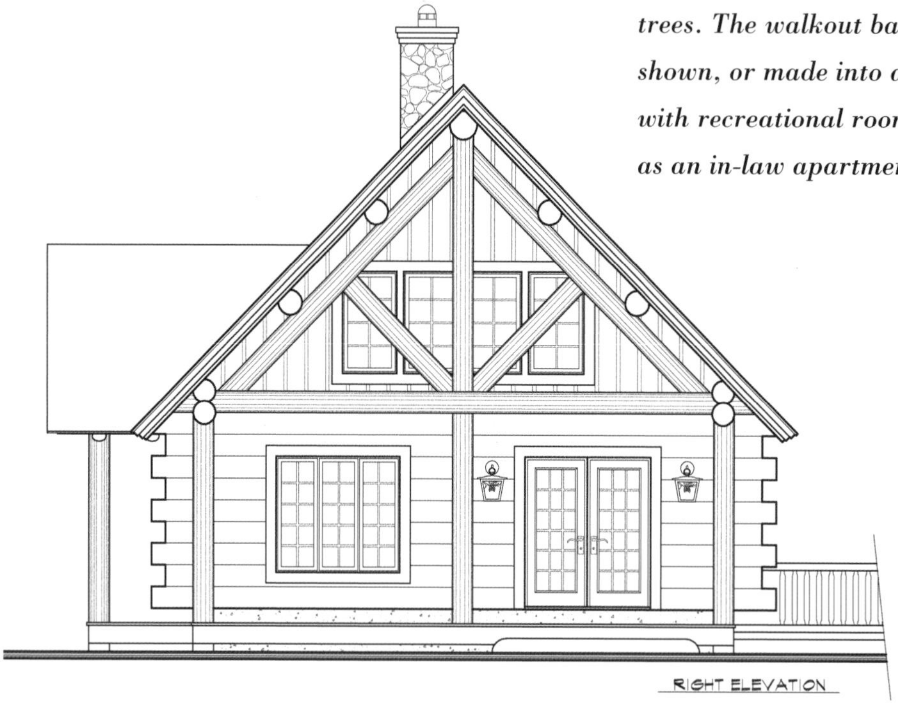

RIGHT ELEVATION

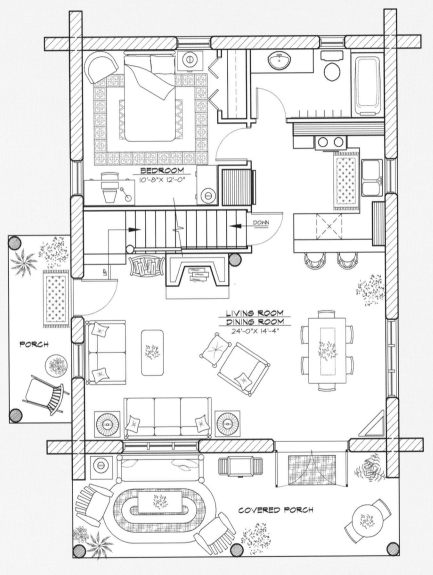

BEDROOM
10'-8"X 12'-0"

DOWN

UP

PORCH

LIVING ROOM
DINING ROOM
24'-0"X 14'-4"

COVERED PORCH

MAIN FLOOR

Blue Herring Bay

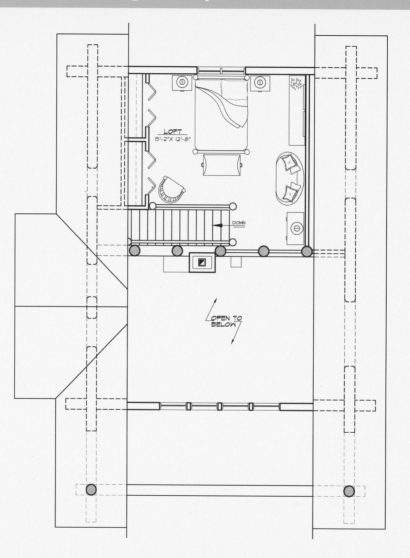

LOFT
15'-2" X 12'-8"

DOWN

OPEN TO
BELOW

2nd FLOOR LOFT

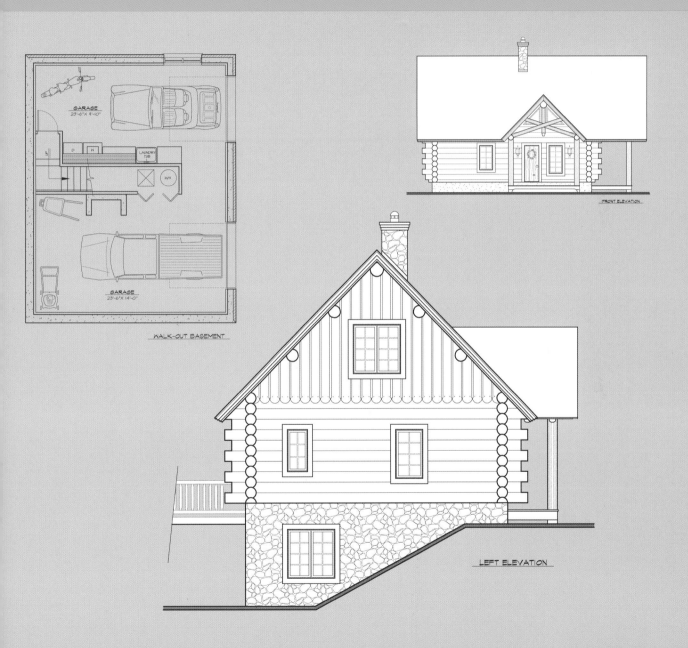

GARAGE
23'-6"X 4'-0"

LAUNDRY
TUB

GARAGE
23'-6"X 14'-0"

WALK-OUT BASEMENT

FRONT ELEVATION

LEFT ELEVATION

Building Small

When you decide to tackle building a log home, consider the fact that your children and family may need more of your time rather than more space in their home. Building a quality smaller home not only allows you to spend more time with your family, it creates spaces that enable you to interact more, making the home seem like a safe haven from our complex world.

Keep in mind that you do not have to get rid of the kids to build a small cabin! There are many "family" advantages to building a smaller home. For one, your family members will be able to spend more time together in shared and open spaces rather than hiding themselves away in solitary areas often created by larger homes. This time together is conducive to family unity and communication, which too many families lack today. Sharing a room can teach a child to be thoughtful and considerate of another's "space" and privacy. It also teaches children to be more organized while learning to live with less.

Cabin living requires a deep search into your soul to find the basics of what you really need in life and to strip away all else. Sometimes you appreciate more by having less, and things that you may have always felt to be important turn out to be unnecessary. This process can become a spiritual quest, as you strip away unneeded baggage and belongings, and simplify your surroundings. It may not be an easy journey. However, you will find the effort extremely rewarding once you discover that you no longer live in the confusion and disarray that can often complicate your life.

Cabin living involves not only learning about building, but also learning about you. Having to choose and analyze your needs is a great

A small but well-planned log cabin creates less of an impact on nature and the environment that surrounds us but can still be spectacular.

TEN SMALL WAYS TO MAKE A
Log Cabin Feel Big

1. Design open and free-flowing spaces to expand the feel of a home.

2. Take advantage of windows—choosing the right window for a space optimizes natural light and extends a room's size. Windows can connect you to the outdoors or make a boring, bland area come to life.

3. Be creative with ceiling heights. Tall, flat, or vaulted ceilings can "raise the roof" on a standard design.

4. Incorporate built-in spaces such as nooks, hutches, drawers, shelves, and other types of storage—these can make the best use of available space in a limited area of the dining room, breakfast nook, seating alcove, etc. Other plans that make efficient use of space are a built-in bunk or a Swedish bed with privacy curtains, a dresser cut out of a sloping knee wall, and a desk or armoire that fills a small nook. Bump-outs and jogs in a structure add architectural interest and, in some instances, provide a more appealing flow to an area without adding a full-sized room. The Swedish-style built-in bed in the Fort Wilderness plan (see page 70) and the Three Bears Inn plan (see page 40) adds great fun and tree-house charm to these cabins.

5. Don't forget the additional unplanned spaces in our basements. Basements can easily be designed to increase the amount of daylight. They can have walkout spaces so they do not feel at all like basements. Using the basement as part of your living space extends the square footage of the main and upper levels and redistributes your useable space. Examples of cabin plans that utilize basement areas are River Dance, Elk Ridge, Fort Wilderness, and Indian Creek. Rather than waste space under the house by using it solely for storage, consider the endless possibilities of this often-forgotten resource. Rethinking the basement area can prove to be a very economical way to carve out additional square footage on a smaller footprint or tight budget.

6. Purchase larger pieces of furniture instead of having a lot of clutter. They will add elegance and balance to the grand-sized log walls of a handcrafted log home.

7. Make closets that are well thought-out and organized. They can easily accommodate two to three times as many items as poorly planned closets and are necessary to keep the small log cabin organized.

8. Create conversation areas in the living room—this area does not need to be big to seat a large number of people. Small conversation areas and groupings of seating space encourage conversation and make a house feel inviting and comfortable.

9. Never underestimate the power of the porch. Porches can extend the home's size for almost three seasons of the year. Put as much time into planning the porch as you do into planning your interior so that the space is inviting, functional, and will be well used.

10. Eliminate unnecessary things. Too much stuff makes a room feel cluttered and robs it of a focal point.

character builder, and may lead to a whole new way of viewing the world.

A poorly planned large home may only give you the illusion of space. Large, expansive spaces can make you feel like you live in a bowling alley, airplane hangar, or cold castle. Smaller, cozier places create a sense of warmth and security.

Using one space for more than one function—sharing spaces—consolidates rooms for a more open, free-flowing plan. When the usefulness and purpose of each space is planned and considered, then a home's design becomes more fluid. We often build homes with rooms for only one purpose, which expands the overall size of the home. A multipurpose floor plan with design flexibility cuts down the number of rooms needed. For example, a separate kitchen, formal living room, and dining room can be combined to save space and make the home feel much larger. A sunroom can double as a bedroom, dining room, or office area. The office can be used as a guest room. The bathroom or kitchen closet can house the laundry facilities. Bunkrooms can be designed into a plan—one room for the girls and one for the boys.

The odd space under the stairs is often forgotten or considered insignificant, but this area can be turned into a real treasure when additional thought is put into its design. Added planning for this area can give character and visual interest to this small space. Some options would be to utilize the last few feet of "unuseable space" of the stairs with site-built deep drawers and/or cubbyholes, indoor wood storage areas, or a built-in phone booth. A child's indoor playhouse can also be creatively carved out of this area, which is a solution that will make you the most popular parent in the world.

© 2003 Rocky Mountain Log Homes

Twig chairs and rush-back seats blend well with a natural log surrounding. The Native American blanket seat cushions and painted furniture are a complementary, bold contrast to the natural materials.

Each small space is an exercise in efficiency. One way to make sure space is being used well is to take an existing plan and thoroughly dissect it to evaluate the use of each room's function and purpose.

Analyze your needs to discover the ways you can obtain the most out of your log home design. Look over and assess each room individually. Consider character, texture, and flow. The challenge in good design is to not only give each room personality, but to develop an efficient use of each and every square inch of space.

The space under the stairs is often forgotten or wasted space. The Tree House Troll plan makes use of the space by designing a children's playhouse or the option of a phone booth, drawers, and shelves.

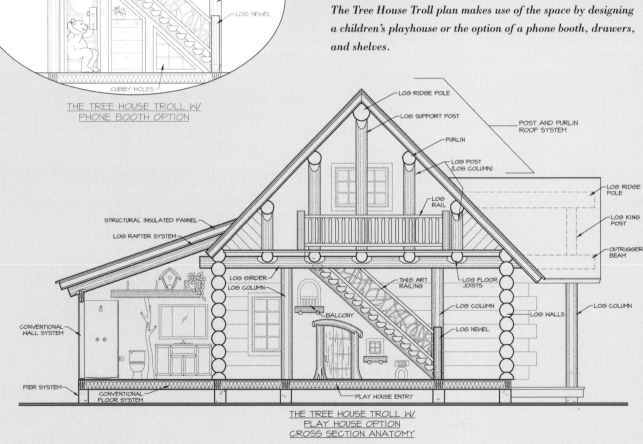

LOG GIRDER
TWIG ART RAILING
LOG FLOOR JOISTS
LOG COLUMN
LOG COLUMN
LOG NEWEL
TELEPHONE
CUBBY HOLES

THE TREE HOUSE TROLL W/
PHONE BOOTH OPTION

LOG RIDGE POLE
LOG SUPPORT POST
POST AND PURLIN ROOF SYSTEM
PURLIN
LOG POST (LOG COLUMN)
LOG RIDGE POLE
LOG RAIL
LOG KING POST
STRUCTURAL INSULATED PANNEL
LOG RAFTER SYSTEM
OUTRIGGER BEAM
LOG GIRDER
LOG COLUMN
TWIG ART RAILING
LOG FLOOR JOISTS
LOG COLUMN
CONVENTIONAL WALL SYSTEM
BALCONY
LOG COLUMN
LOG WALLS
LOG COLUMN
LOG NEWEL
PIER SYSTEM
CONVENTIONAL FLOOR SYSTEM
PLAY HOUSE ENTRY

THE TREE HOUSE TROLL W/
PLAY HOUSE OPTION
CROSS SECTION ANATOMY

*Bedroom retreats become private
sanctuaries from the busy pace of life.*

*A 20 x 20 square-foot cabin is a dollhouse of luxury that
creates the feeling that you are in an estate for a king.*

ABOVE: Small log cabins have a simplicity that with careful thought and planning can transcend time, providing a classic, comfortable feel.

OPPOSITE: The combination of conventional wallboard, stone, and log creates an inviting nook for this bedroom.

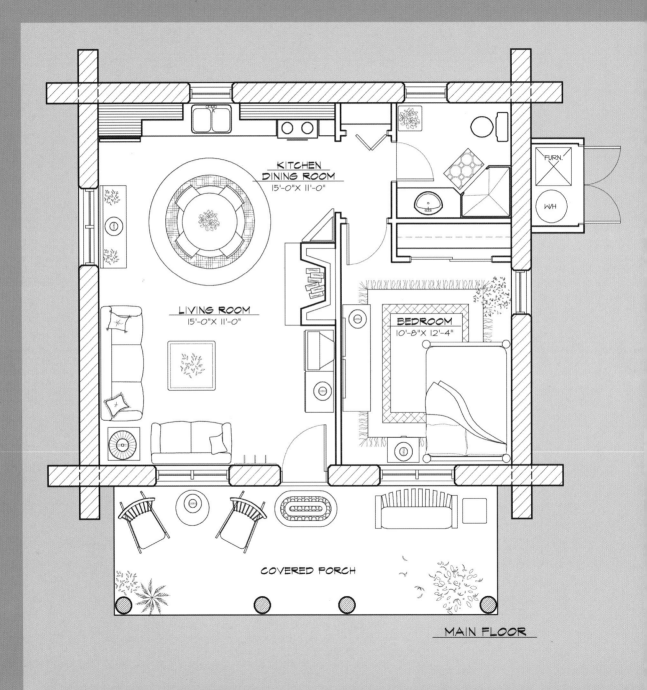

KITCHEN
DINING ROOM
15'-0"X 11'-0"

FURN.

W/H

LIVING ROOM
15'-0"X 11'-0"

BEDROOM
10'-8"X 12'-4"

COVERED PORCH

MAIN FLOOR

Blue Moon

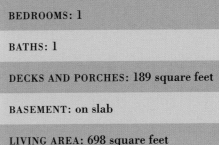

BEDROOMS: 1

BATHS: 1

DECKS AND PORCHES: 189 square feet

BASEMENT: on slab

LIVING AREA: 698 square feet

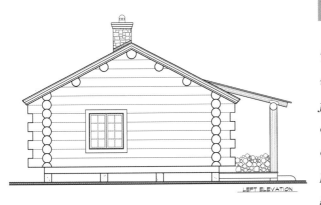

LEFT ELEVATION

This cabin is the picture of traditional cabin life with low pitch roofs, real log gable ends, an open floor plan, and a simple kitchen that still has ample cabinet storage. A good-sized bathroom could be laid out in many different ways to fit your preferences. The bedroom is a comfortable, private getaway from a long, weary day. This log cabin has a lot of living within a small footprint and a great flow of space.

The roof system is vaulted with large log purlins that run straight through the cabin. The mid-span support system within the roof is simple yet carefully woven between the fireplace's chimney.

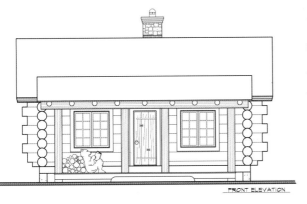

FRONT ELEVATION

Tree House Troll

BEDROOMS: 2 +

BATHS: 1

DECKS AND PORCHES: 339 square feet

BASEMENT: on piers

LIVING AREA: 1,079 square feet

Who said trolls only live under bridges? They also like the useable area under the stairs, as shown in the cross section of this plan on page 30. This roomy log cabin has true tree-house charm. The side covered porch is large with plenty of room for an outdoor dining and lounging area.

The first-floor bedroom has a sunroom feel, wrapped in tall windows. The second floor is left wide open and could be used as a large office, hobby area, poolroom, or an exercise room. Or, by adding a dividing wall, the area could easily be made into two bedrooms.

This open loft is limited only by the imagination.

FRONT ELEVATION

RIGHT ELEVATION

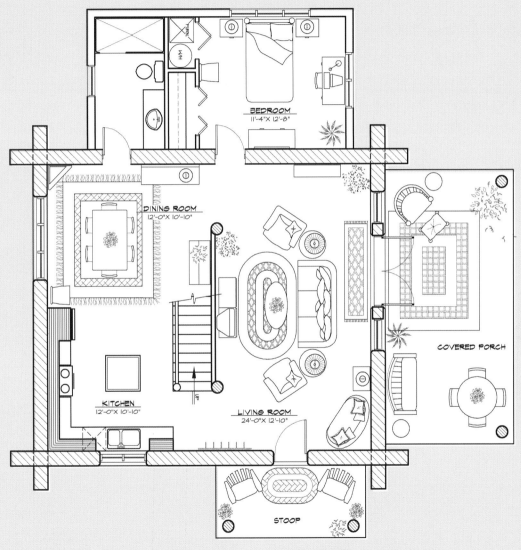

BEDROOM
11'-4"X 12'-8"

DINING ROOM
12'-0"X 10'-10"

KITCHEN
12'-0"X 10'-10"

LIVING ROOM
24'-0"X 12'-10"

COVERED PORCH

STOOP

MAIN FLOOR

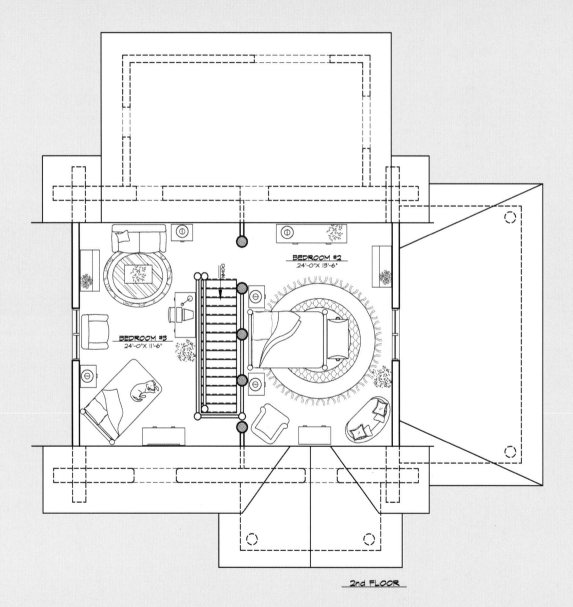

BEDROOM #2
24'-0"X 13'-6"

BEDROOM #3
24'-0"X 11'-6"

2nd FLOOR

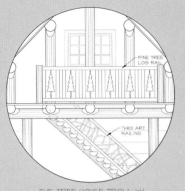

THE TREE HOUSE TROLL W/
PINE TREE RAIL FOR LOFT AND
TWIG ART RAIL FOR STAIRS

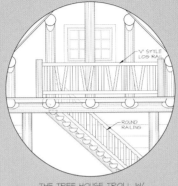

THE TREE HOUSE TROLL W/
'V' STYLE RAIL FOR LOFT AND
ROUND RAIL FOR STAIRS

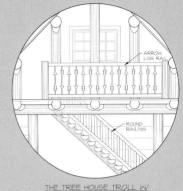

THE TREE HOUSE TROLL W/
ARROW RAIL FOR LOFT AND
ROUND RAIL FOR STAIRS

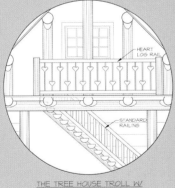

THE TREE HOUSE TROLL W/
HEART RAIL FOR LOFT AND
STANDARD RAIL FOR STAIRS

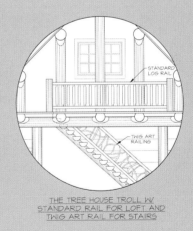

THE TREE HOUSE TROLL W/
STANDARD RAIL FOR LOFT AND
TWIG ART RAIL FOR STAIRS

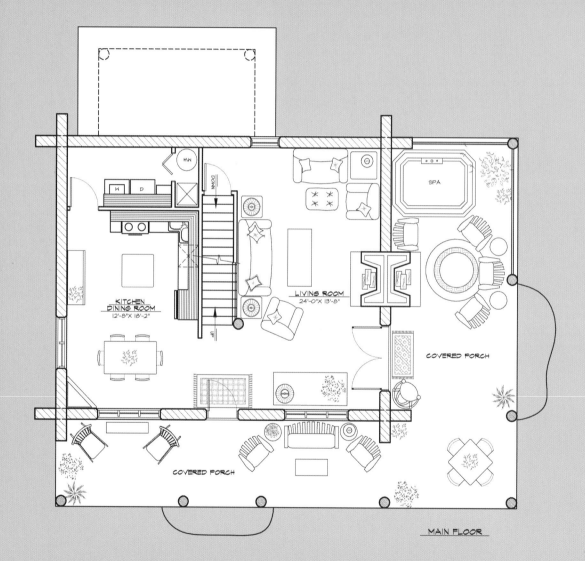

KITCHEN
DINING ROOM
12'-8"X 18'-2"

LIVING ROOM
24'-0"X 13'-8"

SPA

COVERED PORCH

COVERED PORCH

MAIN FLOOR

Three Bears Inn

BEDROOMS: 2, plus bunk

BATHS: 2

DECKS AND PORCHES: 846 square feet

BASEMENT: 829 square feet walkout

LIVING AREA: 1,421 square feet

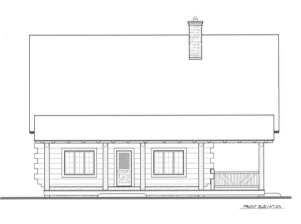

FRONT ELEVATION

RIGHT ELEVATION

This cabin has no shortage of covered porches, as well as log work woven into the roof system everywhere you look. There is the fun of an outdoor fireplace for roasting hot dogs and crisping marshmallows. The living room is perfect for entertaining and has a vaulted ceiling that seems to go on forever.

The second floor has a Swedish-style bed tucked into a bump-out behind the warmth of a curtained wall. The master bedroom has its own private loft that could be used as an office, library, and more.

A bonus of the wonderful basement suite is that it has its own kitchenette. The area is spacious, airy, and open without creating the feeling of being locked away in a basement chamber.

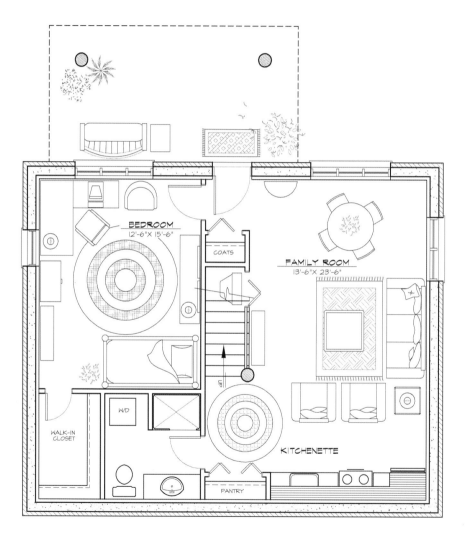

BEDROOM
12'-6"X 15'-6"

COATS

FAMILY ROOM
13'-6"X 23'-6"

W/D

WALK-IN
CLOSET

KITCHENETTE

PANTRY

WALK-OUT BASEMENT

Three Bears Inn

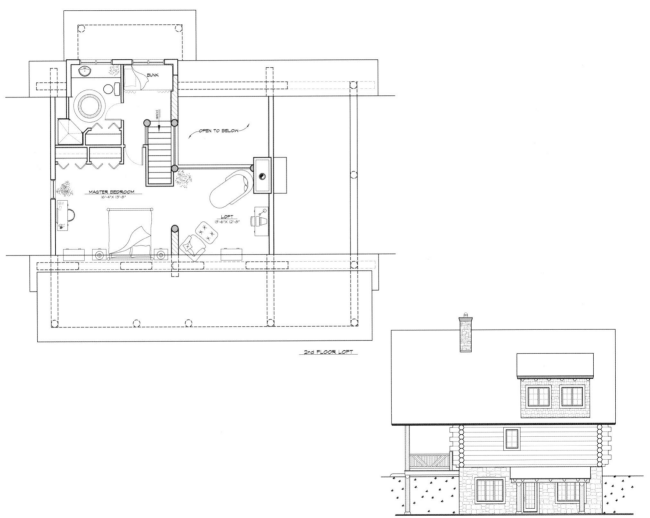

BUNK

OPEN TO BELOW

MASTER BEDROOM
16'-4" X 13'-8"

LOFT
13'-6" X 12'-8"

2nd FLOOR LOFT

BACK ELEVATION

Second Homes: Where and Why to Build

Many people share the dream of building a handcrafted log cabin. The whole concept of a second home is a wonderful idea for those who wish for a carefree lifestyle, and small log cabins have created many great family memories in a charming setting. Although they may be the stuff that dreams are made of, these memories can only be made when all the facts and options are considered.

A second home can be your own personal resort for you and your family for holiday fun and weekend escapes. As such, it makes sense to build in an area you frequent. Once you build you are investing in your own property instead of someone else's; one-month's mortgage payment can often equal a one-week rental fee.

The faraway, secluded cabin in the woods is an advantage for those who have flex time or who are free to take their work with them. This allows them to extend a vacation or a weekend or to take large blocks of

Long-running lengths of ceiling joists are structural components that are not only beautiful, but serve as floor joists that support the rooms above. The lower girder or summer beam acts as a mid-span support allowing more open spanning floor area.

time away from their mainstay. Your frequented second home will likely be closer to home than your typical long-distance vacation destination. And when you consider the time and effort that long-distance travel usually requires, the nearby log cabin appears even more desirable. A typical vacation trip may require a long drive to the airport, then two airline flights, followed by still another 80-mile ride in a rented car with the kids asking over a hundred times, "Are we there yet?" These long distances can easily consume a very long day or more, assuming the weather is good and/or flights are not delayed. These vacations have the potential of adding to the stress and burden from which you already need a vacation.

You may be looking for something that is far from the crowds and soaring costs of some of the more traditional vacation spots. Secluded properties may be inexpensive to purchase. However, be aware that there may be added or hidden costs, such as additional utilities; special engineered septic; long roadways; steep slopes; and sand, clay, or rocky soils that require additional engineering. These added factors may make your dream property cost-prohibitive. The property may appear cheaper because of its remote location, but if you calculate the

The roaring flame of the fire is contained in this fireplace with a pass-through wood storage bin built into the unit's design, which separates the kitchen from the living room.

Courtesy Calija Log & Timber Homes/Napanee Design © 2003 Rob Melnychuk

Vacation Home Tips

1. Consider hiring a team of building professionals. Simple, small cabins are not so simple to build.

2. Remember that cheap land is not always a bargain. Consult with a contractor about general development fees before buying an untamed property.

3. Buy and build because you truly want to enjoy the area and property, not solely as an investment.

4. Make an informed and intelligent buying decision; do not rely on whims and emotion.

5. Talk to friends or family who have a vacation home and ask about their experiences and advice. Don't disregard their negative comments. Consider these comments with an open mind.

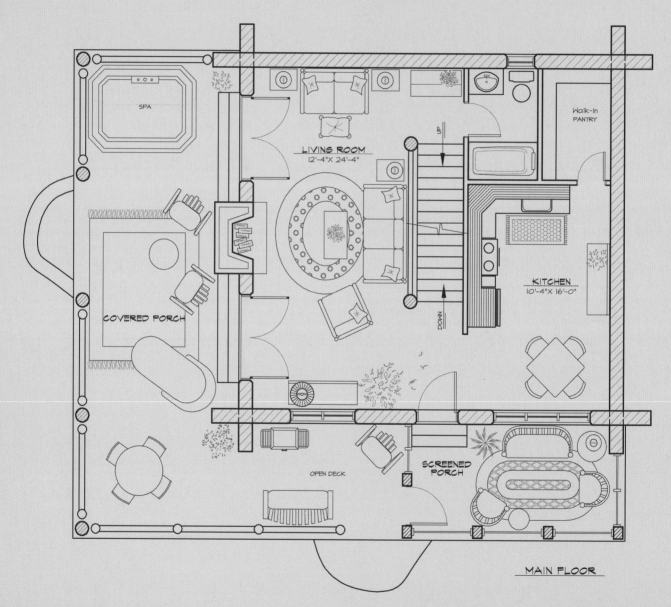

SPA

LIVING ROOM
12'-4" X 24'-4"

Walk-In
PANTRY

COVERED PORCH

KITCHEN
10'-4" X 16'-0"

UP

DOWN

OPEN DECK

SCREENED
PORCH

MAIN FLOOR

Elk Ridge

BEDROOMS: 2 +

BATHS: 2

DECKS AND PORCHES: 630 square feet

BASEMENT: 728 square feet walkout

LIVING AREA: 1,007 square feet

LEFT ELEVATION

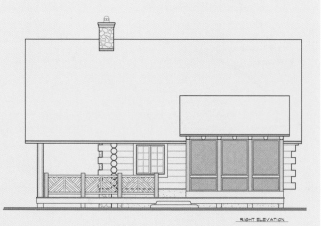

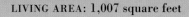

RIGHT ELEVATION

This log cabin classic is loaded with outdoor living. The covered porch extends the living room with a circular flow of large French doors that blur the line between inside and outside. Open areas on the side deck are for barbecues and a touch of sun. A screened-in porch is incorporated for bug-free days and mosquito-free nights.

An oversized living room area is perfect for the family that likes to entertain, and the kitchen has plenty of pantry for all those needed winter provisions. This traditional-style cabin is quite often the design that people think of as the quintessential log cabin.

The walkout basement can be configured in many ways to fit one's lifestyle: a guest apartment, two-bedroom kids' retreat, hobby area, garage, and more.

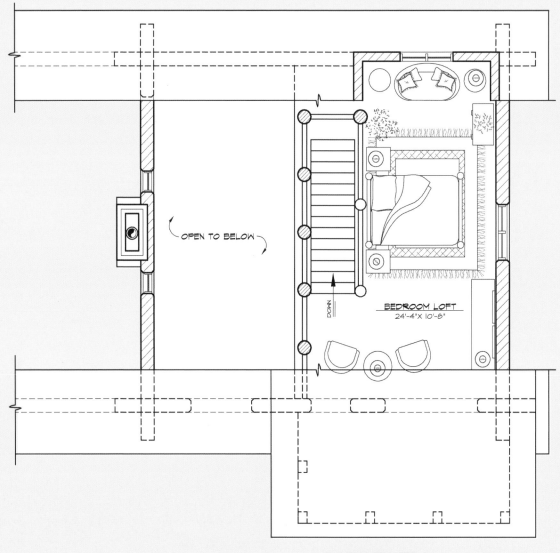

OPEN TO BELOW

DOWN

BEDROOM LOFT
24'-4"X 10'-8"

2nd FLOOR LOFT

Elk Ridge

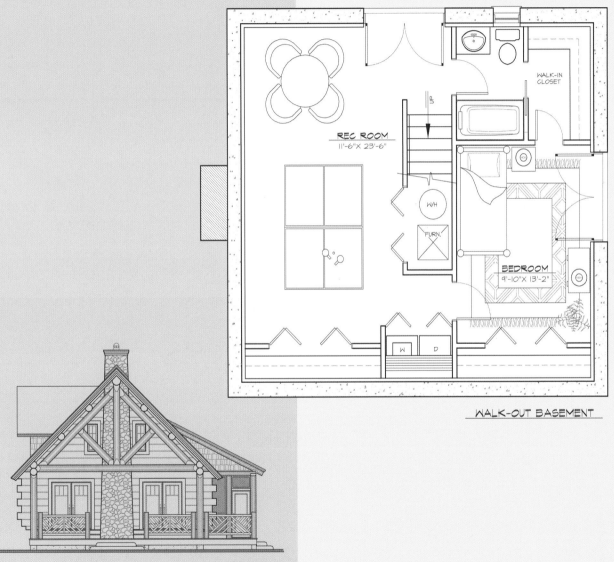

REC ROOM
11'-6"X 23'-6"

UP

WALK-IN
CLOSET

W/H

FURN.

BEDROOM
9'-10"X 13'-2"

W   D

WALK-OUT BASEMENT

FRONT ELEVATION

Designing a home's entry is crucial to the home's overall appeal. This cabin boasts doubled outrigger beams used in combination with king-post supports above the collar-tie.

total costs you may find that this is not the case.

When deciding if you should invest in a log cabin as a second home, you should consider the following:

1. *What are your general interests?*
2. *Are your vacations alone or with family and friends?*
3. *Do you prefer to live your vacation like a hermit where you can get away from everyone and everything?*
4. *Do you want to someday retire at your cabin or continue to visit just periodically?*
5. *Do you want plenty of guest rooms or would you rather avoid altogether the added expense of entertaining?*

If a second home becomes so large that you spend your whole vacation fixing the drains, replacing the hot water heater, repairing the broken screens, and maintaining the structure, property, lawn, and gardens, your plan to have a second home for sheer enjoyment and relaxation has been in vain. You don't want to create a living space that you become a slave to.

These tough and complex issues are enough to give the second homeowner second thoughts. And this is exactly what I want you to do—have second thoughts and take the time to think things through. Most people jump head-first into construction without putting enough thought or planning into it. It is easy and fun to dream, but at some point the dream must convert into reality with careful planning and compromise.

Planning is key to success. Half of the fun of planning is the journey of getting there. Stay focused on the final results. A log cabin is created out of passion as well as solid information. Friends and family will be infected with your "cabin fever" as they bask in the comfort and security that radiates from its four walls. Payoffs like this make the "labor pains" well worth the effort.

Wrapped in windows, the living room has a panoramic view of the lake. The fireplace is capped with a large log hearth and log stubs for added support and interest.

OPPOSITE: Although small in size, this cabin is big on comfort and loaded with details found in a larger estate. The kitchen cabinets, doors, and furniture all have burgundy tones that add contrast and warmth to the natural shade of the log walls.

ABOVE: The mix of mission-style furnishing, antiques, and hand-thrown pottery make this a cabin that feels lived in. The large-size overhead ceiling joists become the support or floor joists for the rooms above.

Willow Creek

BEDROOMS: 2

BATHS: 1

DECKS AND PORCHES: 263 square feet

BASEMENT: on slab

LIVING AREA: 1,042 square feet

The space in this two-bedroom cabin flows, and it blends with nature. The roof system components are combined methods of log and conventional frame building to make the most of the home's design and budget. The log rafter covered porch is laid out to feel warm and cozy, but on a larger scale that allows the most of outdoor life. It also offers an alert dog's command post to guard this log castle's gate.

The conventionally framed roof system and gable ends help to keep the budget in line. The large log ceiling joists are worked into the flat ceiling area to add depth and texture. With this type of ceiling combination, you would never miss the more expensive vaulted ceiling system.

FRONT ELEVATION

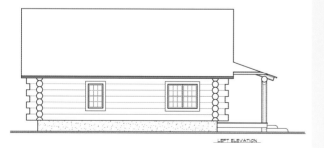

LEFT ELEVATION

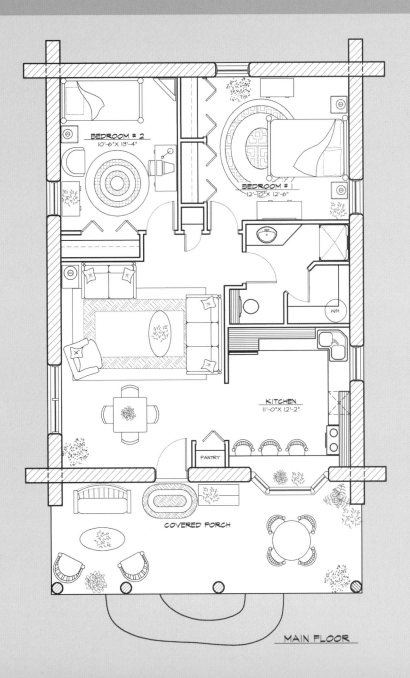

BEDROOM # 2
10'-6"X 13'-4"

BEDROOM # 1
12'-10"X 12'-6"

W/H

KITCHEN
11'-0"X 12'-2"

PANTRY

COVERED PORCH

MAIN FLOOR

Planning Your Log Cabin

Preparing for the major exam of custom building can be a bit of a mind-melter, with its blizzard of documents and endless choices of construction materials. Log home building requires focus and dedication where you must see beyond the surface and sort out your priorities and needs. This is an education of a lifetime where failure is not an option and when one's decisions may be called into question or may cost more than planned. In designing and planning a custom home you can often spend a year or more in research and planning. Be sure to give your project the time and attention it requires and deserves.

A client who is knowledgeable about the process of construction is better prepared. Researching and understanding the building process will give you confidence and success in the choices you make. This does not mean that you have to know each and every trade, but you should have a general understanding of what is involved in building a home in order to sort through and identify what information will be useful to you.

This is more easily achieved with the added guidance of good design professionals on your construction team. Their experience and wisdom

Dining areas separated by the warmth of a fire create interest in this log cabin. The log-ends to the left of the photo illustrate the chink-style log wall system. The "blue stain" on the log-ends is a natural occurrence and can create depth and interest in logs.

is invaluable. Research and knowledge will help you articulate your questions to your design professional and contractor so that your project will reflect your personality and lifestyle while staying within your budget.

DESIGN PROFESSIONALS

Design professionals are often misunderstood, inefficiently used, and/or underused in construction today. A good design professional can lend years of experience to a project, giving a home great value. A specialist in whole-log construction has an understanding and respect for the individual characteristics of the wood and overall construction methods. He or she will understand how the log components and connections affect the cost and structural integrity of the house's framing members.

Once you have survived the test of construction, you can better appreciate the level of detail, planning, and hard work that goes into a quality-built home. The intense thought process is necessary to convey a clear vision of your construction goals to the trades involved and to clarify any issues that will need to be addressed.

FLOOR PLANS VS. CONSTRUCTION PLANS

The floor plan is only a small part of a full construction plan. People often get the two confused. The floor plans you see in magazines and books (such as this one) provide partial blueprints that only show a home's general exterior decor and a room's general location. These plans are not to scale and do not include many details such as log placement, sizes, quality of materials, connections, cross

© 2003 Beaver Creek Log Homes

Not all logs have to be straight in a log home. The perfect log, chosen for its character, can add whimsy to any log cabin.

Doubled purlins supporting the roof system are used here to add strength to the long spanning purlins. A tall stack of log stubs (to the right of the photo) intersect the living room and become the log wall for the dining room beyond.

Long lengths of purlins and ridge poles are supported at the mid-span by a king post (the vertical post). That in turn carries a set of rafter supports, allowing for a more open floor plan. Careful consideration of load bearing and weight transfer must be engineered within a home no matter how small it is.

Hard work is a prerequisite for handcrafted log building.
This form of construction is labor-intensive.

sections, lateral sections, specifications, measurements, and other critical information that full construction plans show. A professional drawing may appear to be nothing more than simple lines that form a house, but there are many elements that have been considered in creating it. A good drawing is much more than a pretty picture and random measurements.

THE IMPORTANCE OF GOOD DESIGN

A good design evolves over time. Stock plans often take many, many years to develop in order to give each plan definition and character. Every square inch is evaluated many times over for efficiency, design, flow, log content, and curb appeal. In planning, the challenge is to find each room's personality, giving attention not only to design but also to its detailed construction content. Every room should be planned so that the family has a reason to use it. The end result is a log cabin that no one can enter without being inspired.

Being completely prepared with full construction plans steps up the pace of construction by giving a clear and direct definition of what you want. Most experienced builders who are organized and efficient do not build or bid projects without blueprints. A good contractor with a professional business is often in high demand. A well thought-out plan is the best way to capture a contractor's attention, because the contractor realizes you are serious about the project and have already put considerable thought into your home.

When drawings are well done, they protect the homeowner from lower-quality materials and vague interpretations of the home's design that can lead to miscommunications and problems of many kinds. The contractor realizes that the blueprint is a full 80 to 90 percent of their contract with the client. Good design drawings are especially crucial to log building, as log craftsmen often complete the structure off-site and never see the job site until the building is being installed on the property.

HOW DESIGN AFFECTS THE SUB-TRADES AND BUDGET

In the design stage, problems are solved and can be turned into assets by finding creative solutions. To design a useable space you have to create functionality where utility and art merge. Your home's design will evolve while in the planning phase. By having carefully thought through the many design choices in advance, you will speed up the conceptual or preliminary drawings process. A carefully crafted design will eliminate guesswork on the part of the designer and tradespeople. Collecting photos, articles, or ads of the things you like and are interested in will help tell the story of your personality and lifestyle so the design professional can build a home that best fits your needs and expectations.

Following the proper design process for even the smallest cabin will help simplify the building process because there will be fewer decisions to be hastily made on-site. A more sophisticated level of design is achieved by developing plans in advance that match your needs and expectations. This will also ensure that your needs are communicated accurately to your contractor. Changing plans on-site can create delays, affecting many trades at a time, which in turn can snowball the cost of a project beyond control.

Modern-day builders are preserving a long tradition of building handcrafted log homes. Here the logs are hand-peeled with the cambium left intact. The cambium is the inner surface of the bark that adheres more to the log during the fall and winter harvesting months. This gives the log what is typically called a "skip-peeled" look.

Risks and Problems

Being aware of the risks and problems that can happen during a construction project will help you steer clear of them. By learning from others' mistakes you can detour away from the most common errors made in building a custom home. Most projects turn out fine with a good team of tradespeople, and building can be a truly rewarding experience when an average design is transformed into an awe-inspiring, spectacular home. Keep in mind the following:

1. *LOG BUILDING IS A VERY DANGEROUS BUSINESS.* The natural beauty of the materials and the calming state of the natural setting can be very deceiving. Life or limb can be gone in a split second with one wrong move or by simply being in the wrong place at the wrong time. There is often not enough time to react quickly. Most loggers' wives are very familiar with the term "widow makers." Be careful!

2. *IT IS SURPRISINGLY EASY* to expand the main walls of a home to the point that you no longer have a cabin, but a lodge. This is fine if it is a lodge you really want. However, homes have a tendency to grow in size uncontrollably when there is no up-front planning on paper. Even on paper it is easy to underestimate how large a space will be. Blueprints can be very deceiving if you do not have years of experience

Carved out of the woods, this log home was carefully considered in design so that the structural elements of a truss were also aesthetically pleasing.

in knowing how to "read" a space. Only then can you be certain what an area will feel like by just looking at a small-scale drawing. Don't let your small log cabin grow out of control.

3. *THE SIZE OF THE HOME* has nothing to do with the price of the structure, especially if it is a small home. Planning to build based on the home's square footage is like buying a car by the pound. There are just too many variables, such as the cost of materials and methods chosen. Believing that one can accurately price a home based on square feet is one of the most common and most dangerous misconceptions of home construction. I see smaller homes that are very expensive because high-quality products are used. By the same token, I've seen many homes that appear very expensive because of a large footprint size with glitz and surface glamour but that are built with pure junk—with a very low cost per square foot.

4. *DON'T MISTAKE QUANTITY FOR QUALITY.* Bigger is not always better. It is the "bones" or structure of a home that counts. Décor is only a surface application. It is the well-engineered home that will stand the test of time.

5. *WISHING WITH ALL YOUR HEART* for the perfect log home does not make your budget grow larger. I know this from personal experience. It is easy to dream beyond the budget, but don't fall into this trap.

6. *RAW LOGS ARE NOT* that expensive to purchase. Finding the right tree, cutting the tree, shipping it to the log yard, debarking, pressure washing, cutting the knots, sanding, and treating the logs is what consumes a lot of money, time, and manpower. Don't let the initial cost of raw logs lure you to forget the real, but often unexpected and hidden, costs of construction.

7. *THE CONSTANT PRESSURE* and outward thrust of a home's roof system is more than it may appear, no matter how small a home is. Engineering is a very important consideration in any form of construction yet these calculations are often unappreciated or disregarded. Engineering a home is sometimes thought of as an expensive option. On the contrary, it may be far more expensive not to have your plans reviewed by a licensed specialist who has an understanding of the specialized trade of log construction.

8. *DO NOT TRY TO CONVINCE YOURSELF* that all plumbers, carpenters, and so on are of the same caliber of crafters. There is a wide range of quality in workmanship in all the sub-trades.

9. *CHEAP BIDS CAN* often translate to low quality and corner-cutting methods and applications.

Intersecting logs from the bump-out gable end add interest to a log home's roof system. The arched-top windows create a focal point and capture the tall views of nature.

Fort Wilderness

BEDROOMS: 2 +

BATHS: 2

DECKS AND PORCHES: 248 square feet

BASEMENT: 858 square feet walkout

LIVING AREA: 1,457 square feet

This log cabin is packed with character and charm. The use of bump-outs, conventionally built additions, twig art, and the combination of materials adds texture and whimsy to this cabin that is "built by nature."

Don't let the cabin's storybook appearance fool you! This home is complicated and labor-intensive to build. The added attention to detail and artistry transforms a simple four-corner log structure into a complex building.

LEFT ELEVATION

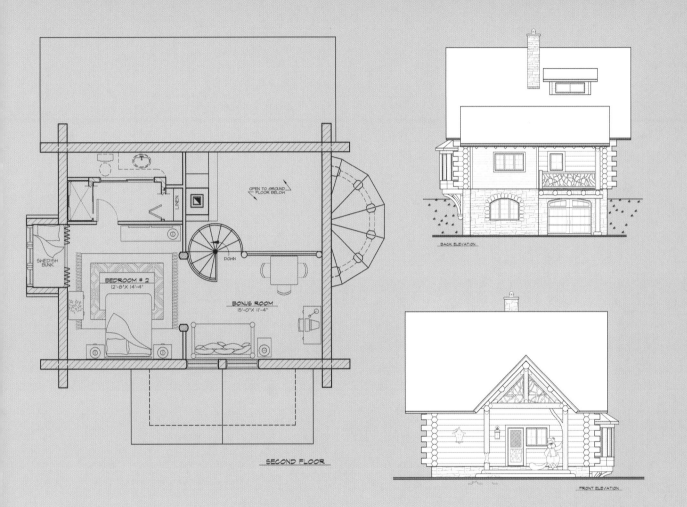

SECOND FLOOR

SWEDISH BUNK

LINEN

OPEN TO GROUND FLOOR BELOW

DOWN

BEDROOM # 2
12'-8"X 14'-4"

BONUS ROOM
15'-0"X 11'-4"

BACK ELEVATION

FRONT ELEVATION

Fort Wilderness

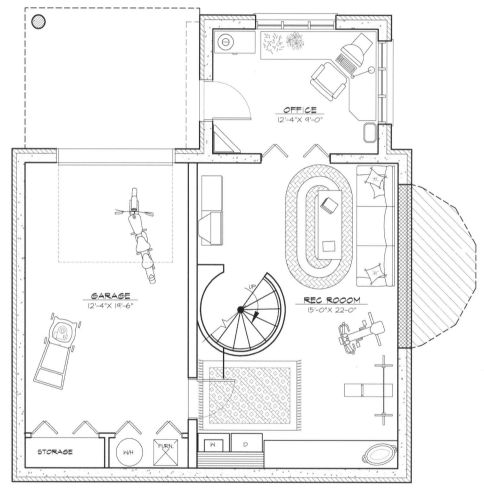

OFFICE
12'-4"X 9'-0"

GARAGE
12'-4"X 19'-6"

REC ROOOM
15'-0"X 22'-0"

UP

STORAGE

W/H

FURN.

W

D

WALK-OUT BASEMENT

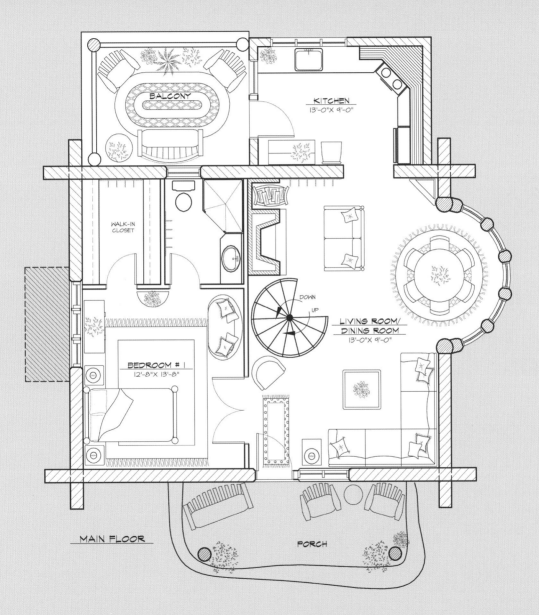

BALCONY

KITCHEN
13'-0" X 9'-0"

WALK-IN
CLOSET

DOWN

UP

LIVING ROOM/
DINING ROOM
13'-0" X 9'-0"

BEDROOM # I
12'-8" X 13'-8"

MAIN FLOOR

PORCH

10. *NOT ENOUGH PLANNING*, unclear focus, and miscommunication are the effects of projects without construction plans. Working with poor construction documents puts everyone at risk. Don't underestimate the importance of construction contracts.

11. *THERE IS USUALLY* not enough time allotted to build a home. Log construction is very labor-intensive. Even seasoned builders can become caught in the trap of underestimating the details, materials, and complexities of a project. A full six to ten months with a full, experienced work crew is needed to build even the smallest of homes. By trying to convince yourself that you can do it in half the time or only on weekends, you will put your project at a high risk of failure. Not that building on weekends can never be an option, but it took us three years of this type of "weekend" construction to build a small 32' x 26' cabin. I vowed never to do that again. A few years later, as the memory of those "labor pains" wore away, we decided to do it again. After all, we reasoned, this time the cabin was only 14' x 17' and we were now much more experienced builders. (And remember, Bob Villa can get a good-sized home done in only seven episodes!) Needless to say, seven years later we are still not done with this "simple" weekend log cabin.

12. *IF YOU ARE A BEGINNER* be sure that you have a good base of schooling in which you read a lot of specialized log building information before attempting even the smallest of log homes. You need to understand that "small" does not always mean simple or cheap to build. There are a few straightforward and nicely illustrated books on the market that address handcrafted log building techniques. One particularly

© 2003 Maple Island Log Homes

ABOVE: Dormers can create a cozy space that houses all types of activities: an office, a playroom, a crafts corner, or an extra bathroom are just some examples.

OPPOSITE: Overstuffed chairs and large fireplaces are great scale-appropriate furnishings for log cabins.

good one is *Log Construction Manual: The Ultimate Guide to Building Handcrafted Log Homes*, written by Robert Chambers. If you do not understand the information in a book like this, then building a log home at all may be a high risk for you, whether or not you have a carpentry background.

13. *IF YOU ARE WELL-READ ON THE SUBJECT,* you will be more focused on your needs. It would be foolish to claim ignorance on the subject of one of the largest purchases you will make in a lifetime. You will eventually be held accountable for your choices—good or bad; you will get out of your log home what you put into it. Learn a good base of information to make educated decisions.

14. MOBILIZATION *AND* DEMOBILIZATION are the construction terms for starting up or closing down a project. This may be on a temporary or permanent basis. These terms do not sound like much, but when it means long lags of time between working on a job site, it can be very expensive and unproductive. It sometimes takes days or even weeks for just one project to regroup. Be aware of the building schedules for your project.

15. *JUMPING THE GUN* and deciding to sort things out later is a "fly by the seat of your pants" form of construction. Not waiting for project cost breakdowns, contractor's or sub-trade's bids and contracts, property surveys, title insurances, or bank loan documents can get you in trouble very quickly. You can sink a lot of money into a project before the real challenges come to light. These are key areas that shouldn't be taken lightly.

16. *THERE ARE MANY THINGS* in the world of construction that take years to learn and master. It is much more complex than most people can imagine. Just because a home is small does not mean you need to know less about construction; building small only feels less intimidating. But there is just as much knowledge needed to build a small home as a large one. What you don't know *can* hurt you. No matter what the size, a great deal of experience is needed to create a home that appears "simple."

17. *A LACK OF PLANNING* creates an inefficient project that is likely to be dragged out over a long period of time. When a project loses momentum and focus, things become much more work than they are worth.

ABOVE: *During the planning stage, think about the sun pattern or direction in siting room locations. Early risers may enjoy the morning sun through the bedroom window to help start the day.*

OPPOSITE: *The use of space and the flow of the design take extra time and planning but are essential to achieve a "simple" cabin with storybook charm.*

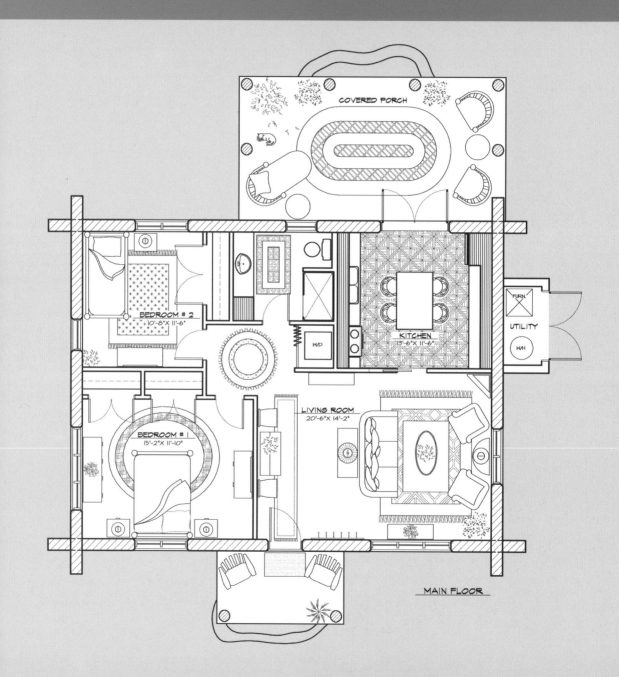

COVERED PORCH

BEDROOM # 2
10'-8"X 11'-6"

KITCHEN
13'-6"X 11'-6"

UTILITY

WD

BEDROOM # 1
15'-2"X 11'-10"

LIVING ROOM
20'-6"X 14'-2"

MAIN FLOOR

Fox Hill

FRONT ELEVATION

LEFT ELEVATION

BACK ELEVATION

BEDROOMS: 2

BATHS: 1

DECKS AND PORCHES: 353 square feet

BASEMENT: on slab

LIVING AREA: 1,096 square feet

This log cabin with a distinctive hip roof is a cost-effective way to avoid the more expensive and labor-intensive full log gable end. The roof adds a beautiful and artful flow to the architectural appeal of the cabin. The conventionally built main roof system can be fast to install while allowing for a large volume of mechanicals in the attic cavity—such as lighting, heat/air, electrical, and speaker systems—all to be hidden from view. There are large logs incorporated into the ceilings that give the wallboard added contrast against the darker log ceiling joists and its flat white surface.

The front and back porches have an interesting combination of log work. The starburst pattern of log fretwork at the main entry adds a rhythm of interest that welcomes you in. The covered back porch is large and inviting and can easily be screened in for those locations where the mosquitoes are as big as birds.

Budgeting and Construction Contracts

The beauty and artistry of building a traditional log cabin is often overshadowed by the reality of the cost and the complexity of today's construction technologies and building code requirements. We must realize (or at least admit) that we are often no longer building simple log cabins—but rather log mansions, castles, and trophy houses. These homes are often filled with expensive furnishings and gadgetry, yet we wonder why it all costs so much and consumes so much of our time. We lose our original purpose and goal and take all the magic and fun out of creating a simple log cabin.

Budgets are closely tied to a home's design. Bumps, jogs, dramatic rooflines, added dormers, or wings incorporated into a simple four-wall system can all add to the cabin's cost. It is not only the initial cost of the structure that can be a big expense. Following the completion of your home, additional expenses include the general upkeep and cost of repairs, such as replacement of roofing materials, added heating costs,

Bright, natural light is ushered in through large banks of windows. Log cabins do not have to be dark, poorly lit quarters. Notice the contrast of the white chinking against the golden-colored logs of this "stack wall" form of cabin construction.

furnishings, window treatments, and unexpected raised taxes, to name just a few.

A tough battle that the contractor must face on every project is to give the client unwanted and sometimes shocking news about realistic budget costs. It is an ongoing frustration when a contractor tries to keep expenses down but must still deal with the high costs of materials and labor in today's market.

In a recent project I was working on with a fellow general contractor who builds quality homes, his pre-construction estimate was so well thought-out that even the glue bottles and pencils were carefully calculated into his line-item printouts. I could relate when he mentioned that "because of the high caliber of work and carefully considered details in my projects, I must often bring a box of tissues and smelling salts to the client's project proposal meeting!" Thank goodness these particular clients we were working with were prepared, realistic, had done their homework, and had a sense of humor! Nonetheless, the projected budget did take their breath away momentarily, but they recovered quickly and calmly asked, "What is it that we might do without that could help bring the budget into line?" The client was realistic and considerate and didn't do what some clients do—that is, expect the contractor to absorb the cost of their inflated dreams. They could see that most of the line items were their choices and not profit for the contractor or sub-trades.

I often see clients rejecting very realistic, quality construction bids basically because they are in denial as to

© 2003 Maple Island Log Homes

ABOVE: This mix of "sticks and stones" is a classic log cabin design. The proportions and balance of the cabin's materials blend well with nature.

OPPOSITE: Only six courses of logs were used to reach a nine-foot ceiling height. These logs were "saddle notched" at the intersecting corners with "chinking" used on the connecting joints.

the true costs and would like the contractor to do their high-end home with a low-end budget. The general contractor's job is a very difficult one, even though a contractor with years of experience can make it look simple.

Many times the contractor who submits a very low bid does not have all of the construction items incorporated into the bid. Or he may have not taken the time to do a thorough cost breakdown and is giving only "guestimates." When this form of bid happens, the contractor is forced to drastically cut quality or materials, or to add future change orders to the client's contract. The client will pay for it sooner or later.

Be prepared to pay fair wages. Pushing the bid too much can compromise the quality of work. The contractor cannot make unrealistic budgets magically work. Adequate compensation for the contractor and sub-trades is in your best interest, as it assures the quality and level of services needed to fulfill the contract. Cost and value go hand in hand.

Hopefully we learn early in the process that we probably can't have it all. The property atop the hillside bluff that overlooks the lake, the beach house that captures views of the breaking waves on the sandy shores,

Wine berry reds are used in the kitchen cabinets, furniture, and accessories as contrasting color against the natural wood tones of the log work. Notice how the ceiling joists intersect the log wall going into the living room. This is the artistry of log architecture in a handcrafted log home.

Low-pitched rooflines make a very warm and cozy atmosphere that has been a traditional hallmark of a log cabin. A large plate of French doors opens up to an outdoor deck that has no shortage of view.

or the home built with large expanses of plate glass, stone fireplaces, and tower rooms all come at a premium price. It is merging the dream with a healthy dose of reality and compromise throughout the process that makes it all work. It is also very important to set an overall budget up front. This will help save a lot of useless wondering and aimless planning.

The home designs in this book are not inexpensive to build. Not much in today's market is inexpensive, especially when one insists on quality. These floor plans incorporate twice the amount of logs into the roof systems, dormers, and porches in order to balance out the weight of the log walls. These special roof systems increase the architectural aesthetics of the log home. Some plans may appear simple but there is actually a great deal of attention to detail, designing, and redesigning of every square inch. Careful design can pack a lot of house into a smaller footprint. Although some of these conceptual drawings may look less intimidating than others, do not let their storybook appearance deceive you about their true complexity.

The closest you will come to knowing a home's cost is by taking a full set of construction plans out to bid. It is a harsh fact that you may not want to hear, but the true cost of construction can only be determined at the time of completion. This uncertainty can cause great anxiety. The best way to avoid any unexpected surprises is to be well informed about your purchase. Do your homework.

Do not expect anyone to hold your hand or give you the magic numbers without a full set of construction plans.

The construction cost breakdown is a very important starting point in any type of construction project. If you choose not to act as your own contractor, you can ask your general contractor to fill it out. The International Log Builders' Association has a great little workbook called *Land to Lock Up*. It will help you sort through your costs and construction goals by providing a line-by-line worksheet of the special items you need to consider in log home construction. It is an easy read with direct and clear information to get you quickly from point A to point B.

Construction documents, also called "contracts," may be the most easily misunderstood and neglected aspect of building any type of home. But they are needed even more than ever in this fast-paced, dollar-driven world. Every year, builders lose thousands of dollars due to miscommunication with sub-trades and the homeowner. Often it is the client who loses in the end because of sloppy contracts that allow loose ends and open interpretations. These losses may be avoided, provided you have a proper and comprehensive contract in place. A signed agreement is your best defense in the event of a dispute. Specialized contracts are more fully explained in a full chapter in my book called *The Not So Log Cabin*. This book also addresses many budget pitfalls and ways to stretch the dollar.

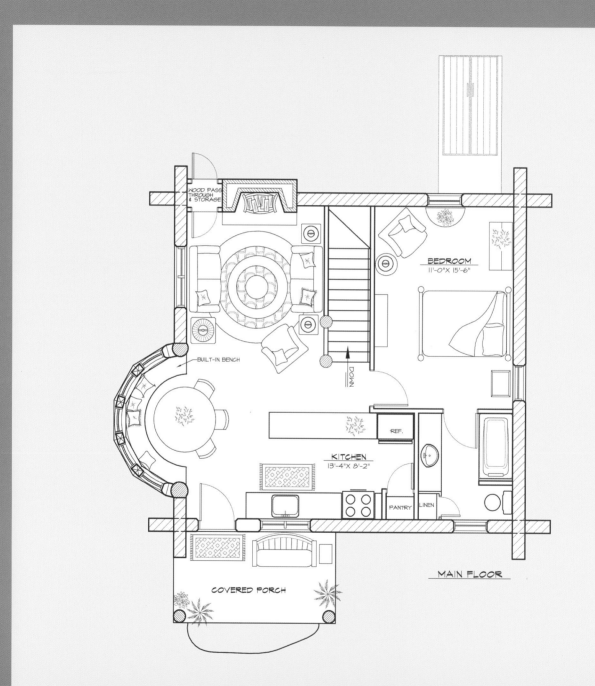

WOOD PASS
THROUGH
& STORAGE

BUILT-IN BENCH

BEDROOM
11'-0"X 15'-6"

DOWN

REF.

KITCHEN
13'-4"X 8'-2"

PANTRY   LINEN

MAIN FLOOR

COVERED PORCH

Indian Creek

BEDROOMS: 2

BATHS: 2

DECKS AND PORCHES: 91 square feet

BASEMENT: 734 square feet

LIVING AREA: 770 square feet

This gracefully arched entry draws you into the cabin, which is designed to fit the most into a very small footprint. The large galley-style kitchen even has a pantry. The built-in dining nook is wrapped into the cabin's design. Overhead log work in the ceiling is carefully considered to add the most visual interest. There is a first-floor bedroom and master bathroom on the main floor.

The daylighted basement incorporates a bunkroom, walk-in closet, full bathroom, mechanical room, washer/dryer facility, and large recreation room. The efficient use of space makes this cabin feel larger than it is.

FRONT ELEVATION

LEFT ELEVATION

RIGHT ELEVATION

Indian Creek

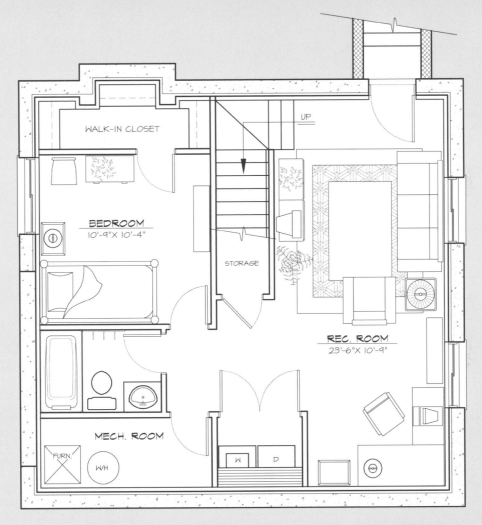

WALK-IN CLOSET

BEDROOM
10'-9"X 10'-4"

UP

STORAGE

REC. ROOM
23'-6"X 10'-9"

MECH. ROOM

FURN.

W/H

W   D

BASEMENT

Moose Lake

BEDROOMS: 2

BATHS: 2

DECKS AND PORCHES: 267 square feet

BASEMENT: on slab

LIVING AREA: 1,053 square feet

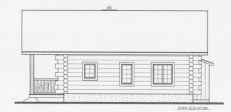

The mix of whole-log construction and timber-frame joinery adds depth and dimension to this log cabin classic. The cattail fretwork pattern is carved into flat, rough-sawn boards then capped with a log handrail and shoe rail. The cattail pattern is included in the full construction drawings.

The main roof system is conventionally built with decorative purlin stubs at the back of the house and log purlins in the roof system at the entry. Whole-log gable ends are used in this home to unify the building's exterior. The conventional roof framing helps support the log gable end for its stability. You will often hear log builders talk about the added expense of a log gable end. It is not just the cost of constructing the actual log work in the gable ends, but the additional engineering, anchoring, and required slip joints that drive this labor-intensive option. In some cases, it is visually worth the expense; in others, it is not missed at all.

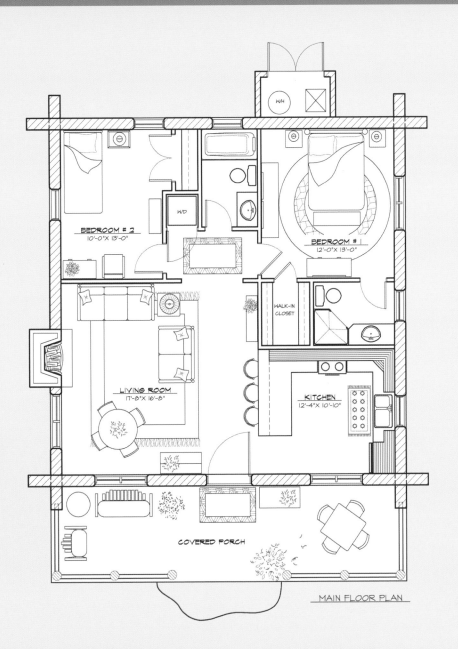

BEDROOM # 2
10'-0"X 13'-0"

W/D

BEDROOM # 1
12'-0"X 13'-0"

WALK-IN
CLOSET

LIVING ROOM
17'-8"X 16'-8"

KITCHEN
12'-4"X 10'-10"

W/H

COVERED PORCH

MAIN FLOOR PLAN

The Log Builder

A handcrafted log home is often selected for its unique-ness, sculptural form, function, and high-quality work-manship. It is easy to see the care and sensitivity that goes into each and every cut log. There is an ever-present energy that radiates from the caring touch of many hands, which builds value into a simple log cabin. Discipline, hard work, and an appreciation for natural materials are prerequisites for being a handcrafted log builder. To work in harmony with nature, one must be able to accept the natural imperfections of raw materials and learn how to work in harmony with them. When individuals have a true love of their art, they put their souls into their work. They often lose all sense of time as they create their art. A true handcrafted log builder is born with a little woodchuck in her soul and a lot of sap in her blood.

Mastering the world of handcrafted log building demands patience and dedication. Logs are a living, breathing element with natural dynamics and properties that are not familiar to most people. Many of the materials are raw, organic substances that command the owners' and builders' reverence and respect. A knowledge of the power of Mother Nature is essential even before the first log is cut. The hand-crafted log home is built in a tradition where integrity and ingenuity are part of the log builder's daily life. These artisans work hard in order to make it appear simple. The log builder often possesses a resourceful nature and way of life that involves constant sacrifices.

The large, open loft showcases the complex roof log work with a combination of trusses, purlins, ridge poles, and miles of log railings. The stairs to the left climb three floors with an open design—they serve as the cabin's own built-in Stair Master.

Because years of experience are needed to master the art of log building, prospective buyers reap far greater value than they may know for the amount of hours, skill, and artistry that is invested in a handcrafted log structure. Although rustic in nature, today's log home is far from unsophisticated. Many of the tools still used in the construction of a handcrafted log home are quite medieval in appearance and may seem primitive in this computer age. This slow and traditional method of building is still the best way to create a handcrafted log home. Each hand-peeled component of a log home is meticulously scribed and pieced together like a jig-saw puzzle to ensure a sculptured fit. The modern-day masters are preserving a tradition that was nearly lost not so long ago.

A large majority of handcrafters have very small operations, as it is difficult to deal with the general business details generated by running a large company. Often a main purpose for a builder in deciding to build log homes is to be in solitude with nature. It is very typical for a handcrafted log builder not to have a receptionist, sales staff, accountants, or in-house design professionals. Most handcrafted log builders never advertise in magazines, on television, radio, or in phone books. Don't be shocked or expect that these are criteria for a "good" log craftsperson. The key is to find a person or company that has experience in log building, a good reputation, and in whom you have confidence and a comfortable rapport.

BELOW: Dovetail joinery toward the roofline is done with a "chinkless" or scribed fit method of log construction. Although the lines appear clear and simple, the level of complex joinery is far beyond the beginner's scope of work.

The bold choice of fabrics against natural materials creates a cabin with kick.

This small vacation cabin is enough to make you forget the large home you left behind.

Whitewashing the walls brings out the grain in these large-diameter logs.
The conventional partition can be a great contrast to all the woodwork
in a log home and can be treated in many different ways.

The owners of this small mountaintop cabin gave up their large home to live here where they would have more time for their hunting and sporting gear business, as well as more time for family and friends. Built in the '70s, the finish work on the cabin was done over time by both owners.

The fluid movement of these spiral stairs is artwork on its own. The craftsmanship and sturdy mortise-and-tenoned joinery may appear simple, but it takes years of experience and patience to master.

River Dance

BEDROOMS: 3

BATHS: $2\frac{1}{2}$

DECKS AND PORCHES: 920 square feet

BASEMENT: 1,108 square feet

LIVING AREA: 1,305 square feet

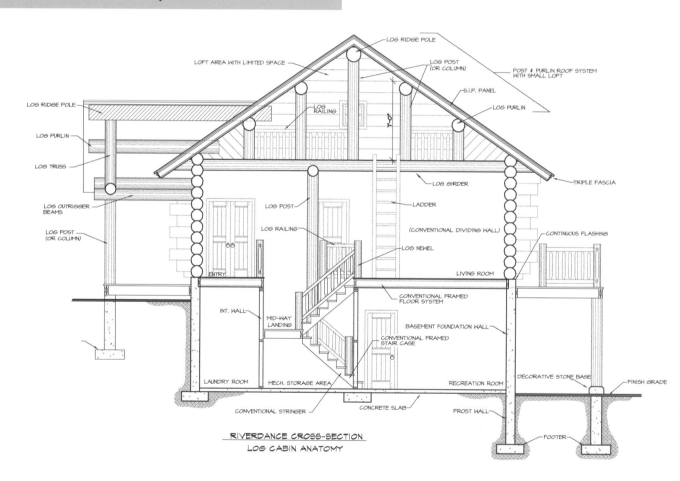

RIVERDANCE CROSS-SECTION
LOG CABIN ANATOMY

This cabin was inspired by a client who wanted something very similar to the Wolf Ridge design from my first book, Small Log Homes. She loved the general idea of Wolf Ridge's base plan, but wanted to customize it for her lifestyle. She sent me her wish list for the main floor and the basement along with a few sketches of what she saw the areas might possibly fit. We played with the layout a few different ways and spent added time tweaking the plan and possible options. The client's careful design consideration and intense thought process combined with our design experience, and gave birth to a whole new floor plan.

The cabin overflows with outdoor living. Its design is loaded with architectural details and personality that you typically see in old lodges. These creative, traditional details add interest as well as extra cost to a "simple" structure. The cabin was doubled in size by the use of a walkout basement with two bedrooms, laundry, full bathroom, a large recreation room with juice bar, and a light-filled basement.

RIGHT ELEVATION

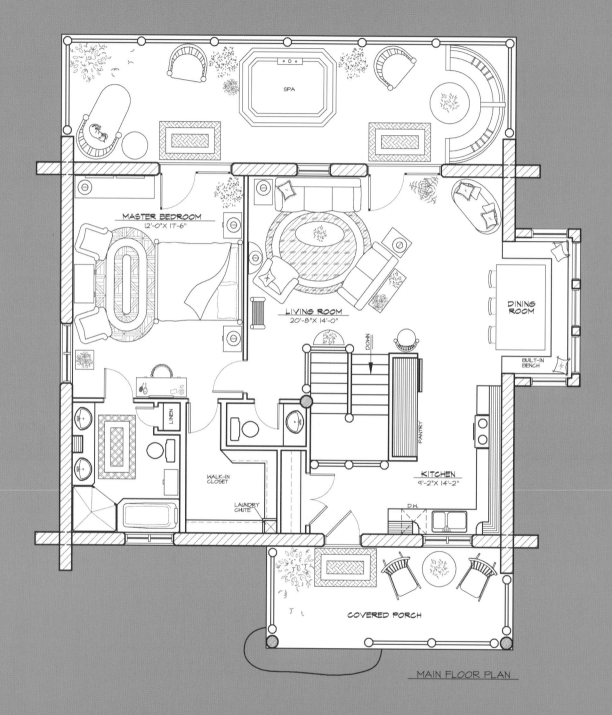

SPA

MASTER BEDROOM
12'-0"X 17'-6"

LIVING ROOM
20'-8"X 14'-0"

DINING
ROOM

BUILT-IN
BENCH

DOWN

PANTRY

LINEN

WALK-IN
CLOSET

LAUNDRY
CHUTE

KITCHEN
9'-2"X 14'-2"

D.W.

COVERED PORCH

MAIN FLOOR PLAN

River Dance

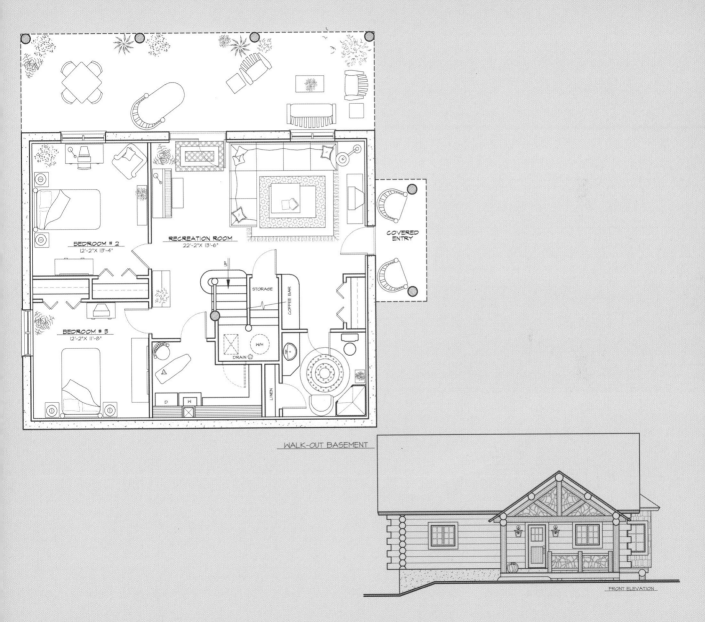

BEDROOM # 2
12'-2"X 13'-4"

RECREATION ROOM
22'-2"X 13'-6"

COVERED
ENTRY

BEDROOM # 3
12'-2"X 11'-8"

STORAGE

COFFEE BAR

UP

DRAIN

WH

LINEN

D   W

WALK-OUT BASEMENT

FRONT ELEVATION

Saltbox Garage

484 square feet

This New England saltbox roofline has a classic shape. The two-car bay is perfect for additional storage of garden tools, lawn equipment, boat storage, or the perfect cover for the Harley as a comfortable "hog" house (which fits right in with the flying pig weather vane).

The side door allows quick access. Inside there is a pull-down ladder to a small attic storage area. The extended roofline creates a great area for wood storage. The garage doors can be on hinges like a traditional garage or barn door, or can be modified and adapted to a one-door unit in combination with an electric garage door opener.

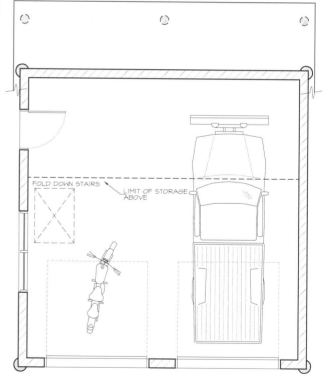

FOLD DOWN STAIRS

LIMIT OF STORAGE ABOVE

TWO CAR GARAGE

FRONT ELEVATION

LEFT ELEVATION

Reclaimed Wood

Salvaged or reclaimed woods are gaining respect and appreciation from homeowners and builders. A heightened sense of responsibility to protect our valuable natural resources goes hand in hand with our growing appreciation for rescued building materials.

Reclaimed woods are rescued from nineteenth-century factories, rural and urban homes, trestle bridges, and maritime structures. These materials are given a second chance for a purpose. The transformation begins as the wood is collected, resawn, replaned, and then graded. The final product is beautiful wood flooring and boards that are coveted for their wormholes, weathering, blue-stains, knots, and nailing marks. These time-weathered features contribute to the wood's character and effect. The current market trends lean toward new materials, so it is an ongoing struggle to educate the public on the dynamics, characteristics, and added beauty of natural and reclaimed resources. Like a fine wine, these properties evolve over many years where the wood is aged to perfection.

It is an art and a challenge to build with recycled materials and architectural pieces, yet it is a challenge that will prove most rewarding. Good craftsmen realize that old structures were built with high-quality materials and loving craftsmanship and want to preserve these historical treasures. They would rather breathe new life into old materials than dispose of them.

Another draw of worn wares is that they have mystery and charm; there is always a story behind each piece. What type of structure was the

Nineteenth-century antique log homes are disassembled, then reassembled on a new site. Heart pine beams and remilled flooring are all part of the "new" home package that is lovingly restored for another generation of log home enthusiasts.

ABOVE: Log rafters repeat a pattern overhead. The bed and dresser are newly crafted out of old recycled wood.

OPPOSITE: A cabin's kitchen can be simple or more complex. This cabin's floors, walls, furniture, doors, and ceiling are all made of recycled materials.

material salvaged from? Where or what country did it come from? When was it reclaimed? Reclaimed historic treasures from old buildings in Russia to old barns in New England, to a Canadian warehouse or a trestle bridge from the rugged terrain of the Wild West are only a few of the many interesting past lives these materials may have lived.

Reclaiming History

To take something of the past and bring it to the future with someone that appreciates and understands old and recycled materials is a talent of its own. The artisan who chooses salvaged materials expects small imperfections. He or she appreciates and celebrates the beauty of natural wear. Working with a salvaged piece will take additional effort, but the finished result can be stunning with a patina that will often outshine any new piece.

We are often too quick to discard items that still have a life to live. There are professionals and hobbyists who have the patience and knowledge to give added life to old stoves, refrigerators, televisions, radios, hardware, barns, and log cabins. They enjoy these "rebirths" of valued treasures that can be passed on to a new generation of caretakers who collect and preserve these pieces of history. To rescue a salvaged piece of material, whether it is flea market funk, a junkyard find, or a hand-me-down creates a unique fusion of old and new. The results are whimsical furnishings, vintage looks, or a complete return to the original spirit of an item where the passage of time only adds to its beauty.

OPPOSITE: A cozy room, with the warmth of a fire to tell a good story by, is a great place to gather after a hard day's work.

OPPOSITE: A comfortable bedroom loft among the rafter roof system has a canopy of log work overhead. Reclaimed floorboards, ceiling, rails, and furniture create a warmth that is hard to re-create in new materials.

RIGHT: Simple beauty is the statement made by this bathroom. The tub stands on its own as a work of art.

BELOW: This reclaimed old dovetail structure was dismantled, shipped, and reinstalled on its new location. Many years of planning, restoration, and loving care went into bringing new life to this abandoned old structure.

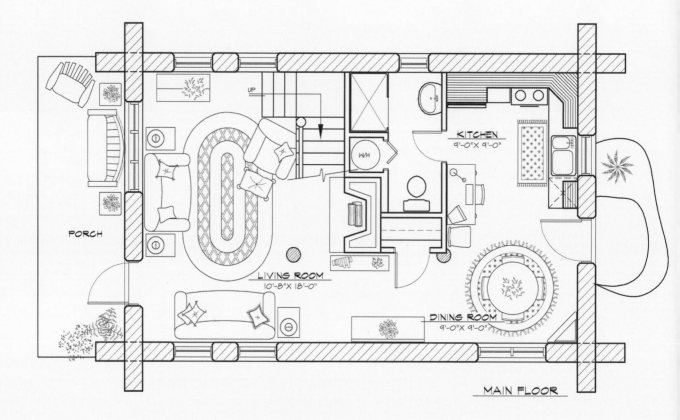

PORCH

UP

LIVING ROOM
10'-8"X 18'-0"

W/H

KITCHEN
9'-0"X 9'-0"

DINING ROOM
9'-0"X 9'-0"

MAIN FLOOR

Wind Cliff

BEDROOMS: 2 +

BATHS: 1

DECKS AND PORCHES: 116 square feet

BASEMENT: on slab

LIVING AREA: 1,332 square feet

This country cabin is extremely comfortable and homey. The log walls run high, creating a knee wall in the second-floor bedrooms. There is a lot of log work incorporated into the roof and wall systems to create bedrooms that feel like tree-house hideaways.

FRONT ELEVATION

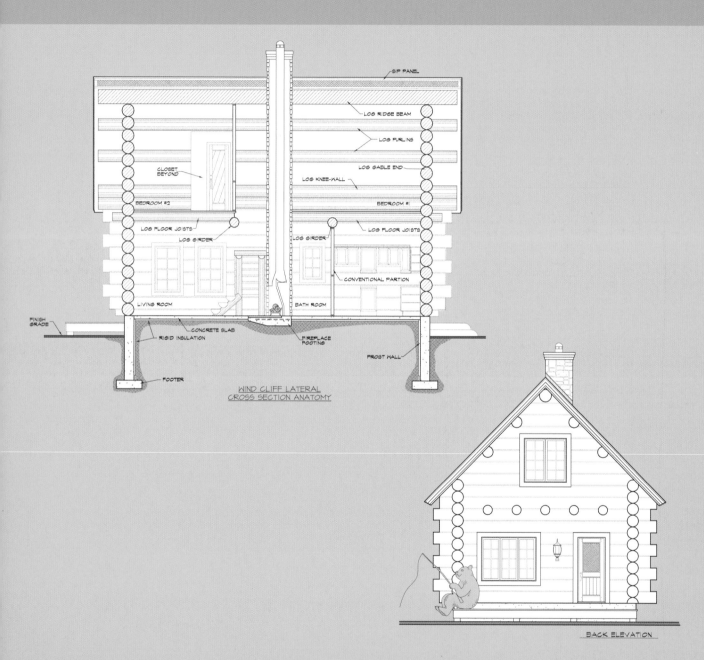

SIP PANEL

LOG RIDGE BEAM

LOG PURLINS

LOG GABLE END

CLOSET
BEYOND

LOG KNEE-WALL

BEDROOM #2

BEDROOM #1

LOG FLOOR JOISTS

LOG GIRDER

LOG GIRDER

LOG FLOOR JOISTS

CONVENTIONAL PARTION

LIVING ROOM

BATH ROOM

FINISH
GRADE

CONCRETE SLAB

RIGID INSULATION

FIREPLACE
FOOTING

FROST WALL

WIND CLIFF LATERAL
CROSS SECTION ANATOMY

BACK ELEVATION

Wind Cliff

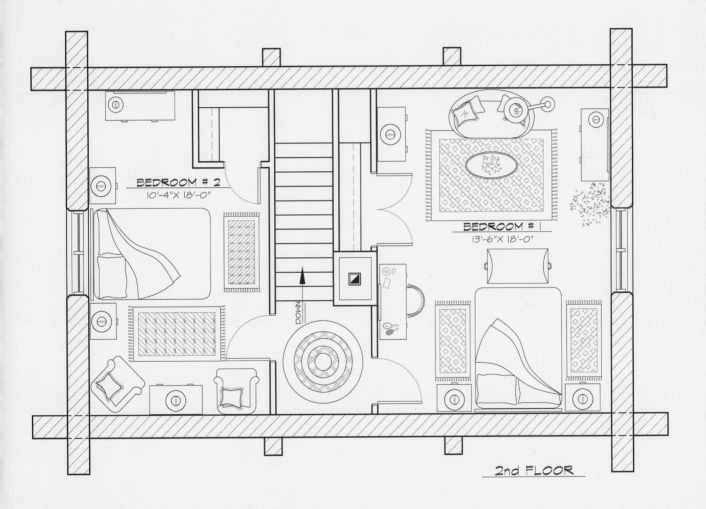

BEDROOM # 2
10'-4"X 18'-0"

BEDROOM # 1
13'-6"X 18'-0"

DOWN

2nd FLOOR

Yellow Pines

BEDROOMS: 2

BATHS: 1

DECKS AND PORCHES: 263 square feet

BASEMENT: on slab

LIVING AREA: 1,047 square feet

The arched covered entry of this log home is very welcoming. The two large bedrooms are full of closets and share a bath and a hallway laundry room.

The cabin roof system is built with conventional framed rafters and a board-and-batten gable end with wood pegs that stand proud. The conventionally framed roof is a great money saver. Log ceiling joists are used to add mass and architectural interest to the flat ceiling area.

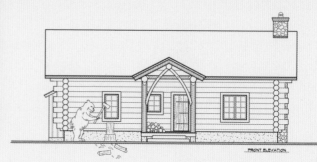

FRONT ELEVATION

BACK ELEVATION

RIGHT ELEVATION

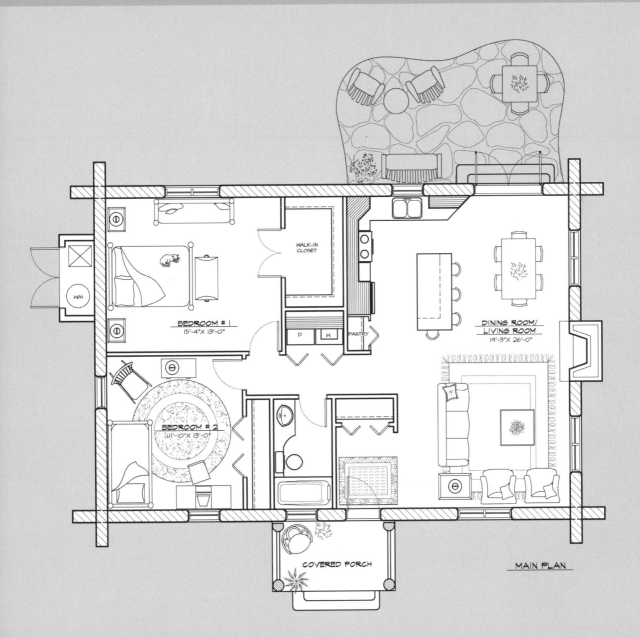

WALK-IN
CLOSET

BEDROOM # 1
15'-4" X 13'-0"

D   W

PANTRY

DINING ROOM/
LIVING ROOM
19'-3" X 26'-0"

WH

BEDROOM # 2
11'-10" X 13'-0"

COVERED PORCH

MAIN PLAN

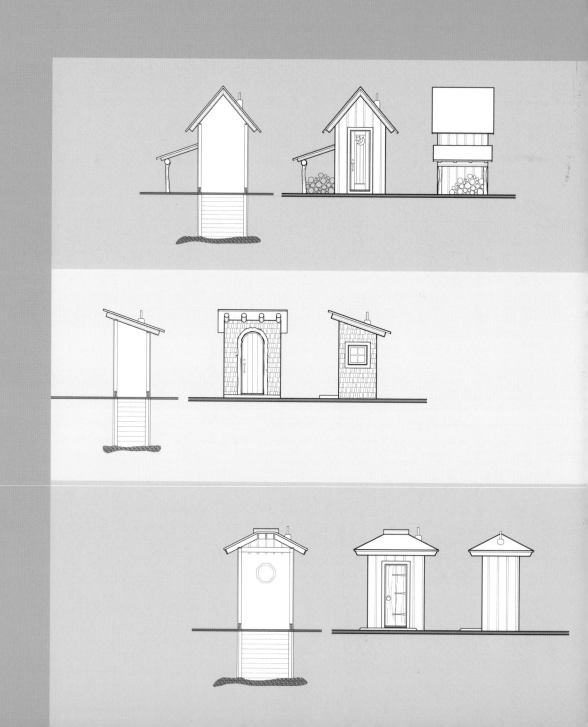

The Royal Flush

Outhouse

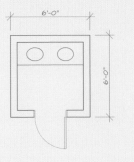

Hey, don't laugh! Bathrooms are one of the highest ticket items in home construction. An outhouse can be a creative solution for the influx of houseguests. At the very least, it gives the neighbors something to talk about!

Outhouse architecture can be an art in itself. We built ours out of the firewood scraps from the construction site. Building an outhouse could be a great weekend or holiday project that can be done as a family or could harness some of that neighborhood teenage energy.

NOTE: *Be sure to check with your local code requirements. Not all areas allow outhouse construction.*

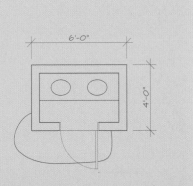

Momma and baby bear are carved out of log stumps to create interest in a garden of full pines.

Building
with Nature

 Homeowners today have the buying power to influence building methods and architecture, which will have an enduring impact on future generations. We can leave a legacy of craftsmanship and artistry for all to enjoy. Smaller, more carefully considered structures could greatly minimize the damage to our environment. Quality buildings, not pretentious and grandiose structures, will age to perfection with less negative impact on our children's future. Building in harmony with nature is the awareness and consideration of the environment around us and the realization that we cannot improve on Mother Nature's artistry. People typically choose to build a log cabin in remote locations because they love to surround themselves with nature's delicate and expansive beauty.

Home building for a better future will require a collective effort to end the cycle of fast-track, substandard construction methods and building practices that create "disposable housing." These rapid, sub-quality construction techniques require the use of hazardous chemicals. These hazardous chemicals wrap our homes into "chemical cocoons," quite often and unknowingly affecting our most precious gift—good health. Building more environmentally safe housing requires some self-evaluation that may mean peeling through the layers of what is truly important and knowing that it may

Bears like these designed by Steve Joslyn are strong and playful design elements to add to any log cabin décor. Sketches are courtesy of Joslyn Fine Metalworks.

This primitive furniture was created out of the log cutout scraps rescued from the firewood pile. They were transformed into a table and stub chairs for the guests at this rental cabin overlooking Lake George in the beautiful Adirondack Mountains.

take compromises in our lives to achieve the goals of building with more "green" methods. Thankfully, some architects, builders, and large industries are also beginning to see the value of building green structures.

It takes a lot of energy and resources to create new synthetic materials. Some building materials are specially treated to make the product last for years, but these chemicals and toxins eventually leech off into our environment. These chemical components often do not naturally or easily break down, and they deposit toxins for many generations. We are not aware of all the long-term effects these products leave, and they often have no smell, taste, or visible warning to alert us. Just because a product or material is produced, or we are told at this point in time that it is "safe," does not mean we should not give each item additional thought, research, and consideration to the application in our homes. Less processed building materials are more naturally balanced. When they have served their life's purpose, they can return to the earth without fear of what they have left behind.

As caretakers of our planet, our best legacy for future generations is that we try to be guardians of our natural resources and our beautiful but delicate world.

Resources

INTERNATIONAL LOG BUILDING ASSOCIATION
PO Box 775
Lumby, BC V0E 2G0 Canada
www.logassociation.org
[250]547-8776
[800]532-2900
The Log Building Association web site lists hundreds of traditional handcrafters from all over the world. Many listings are never seen within the standard log-building magazines.

LOG HOME GUIDE
PO Box 671
1107 NW 4th Street
Grand Rapids, MN 55744-0671
www.loghomeguide.com
[888]345-LOGS (5647)
A special-issue magazine with a hand-selected list of the top one hundred log builders in North America. A valuable resource list of hand-crafted log builders within your region and around the world. This is not a list collected by invitation only, and is not by paid advertisers.

CROWN POINT CABINETRY
153 Charlestown Rd.
Claremont, NH 03743
[800]999-4994
www.crown-point.com
Period-styled cabinetry, handcrafted to the finest quality finishes and within the tradition of master craftsmen and artisans.

Blueprint Price Information

The plans in this book can be purchased from:
BEAVER CREEK DESIGN SERVICES
35 Territory Road, Oneida, NY 13421
www.beavercreekdesignservices.com
[315]245-4112

Garage Plans:
5 Sets: $325.00   8 Sets: $375.00

Small Log Cabin Collection (under 999 sq. ft.):
5 Sets: $485.00   8 Sets: $535.00

Storybook Log Homes Collection (1,000–1,999 sq. ft.):
5 Sets: $745.00   8 Sets: $796.00

ALL PRICES ARE SUBJECT TO CHANGE WITHOUT NOTICE.

All prices are subject to shipping and handling costs. Orders should be made carefully. All plans are specifically printed for each client with no refunds available.

CONKLIN'S
RD #1, Box 70
Susquehanna, PA 18847
www.conklinsbarnwood.com
[570]465-3832
Authentic antique barn wood and hand-hewn beams. A new tradition of reclaiming and honoring the history of wood.

LOG CONSTRUCTION MANUAL
The Ultimate Guide to Building Handcrafted Log Homes
Robert Chambers
Deep Stream Press
Distributed by Chelsea Green
Publishing Co.
ISBN 0-9715736-0-3
[800]639-4099
Knowledgeable, clear and direct information to make it easier for new log builders to have meaningful and dependable guidelines for handcrafted log building construction methods.

YESTERTEC DESIGN COMPANY
PO Box 190
Center Valley, PA 18034
[610]838-1194
www.yestertec.com

LAKE PLACID LODGE
Whiteface Inn Rd.
Lake Placid, NY 12946
[518]523-2700
www.lakeplacidlodge.com

JOSLYN FINE METALWORK, INC.
1246 Rt 80
Smyrna, NY 13464
[607]627-6580
www.usblacksmith.com

WALDEN LOG HOMES
PO Box 366
Lookout Mountain, TN 37350
[423]821-8070
www.waldenloghomes.com

BEAVER CREEK LOG HOMES
35 Territory Rd.
Oneida, NY 13421
[315]245-4112
www.beavercreekloghomes.com

MAPLE ISLAND LOG HOMES
5046 SW Bay Shore
Suttons Bay, MI 49682
[231]271-4042
www.mapleisland.com

ROCKY MOUNTAIN LOG HOMES
1883-L Hwy 935
Hamilton, MT 59840
[406]363-5680
www.rmlh.com

ACKERMAN HANDCRAFTED
LOG HOMES INC.
PO Box 1318
Carbondale, CO 81623
[970]963-0119

DURFELD LOG CONSTRUCTION LTD.
530 Sunset Drive
Williams Lake, BC V2G 2Y9 Canada
[250]989-0555

CALIJA LOG & TIMBER HOMES, LTD.
PO Box 1954
100 Mile House, BC V0K 2E0 Canada
[250]395-8881

NAPANEE DESIGN, LTD.
4922 Marine Dr.
West Vancouver, BC V7W 2P4 Canada
[604]913-3193

LEGENDARY LOGCRAFTERS
Box 133
Collingwood, ON L9Y 3Z4 Canada
[705]444-0400
www.legendarylog.com

STAIR MEISTER LOG WORKS
5854 Rawhide Ct., Suite A
Boulder, CO 80302
[303]440-2994
www.logstairs.com

PEDERSEN LOGSMITHS, INC.
PO Box 788, Hwy 93N
Challis, ID 83226
[208]879-4211
www.pedersenlogsmiths.com

TIMMERHUS, INC.
3000 N 63rd St.
Boulder, CO 80301-2935
[303]449-1336
www.timmerhusinc.com

JEAN STEINBRECHER ARCHITECTS
PO Box 788
Langley, WA 98260-0788
[360]221-0494
jsa@whidbey.com

TROUT HOUSE VILLAGE RESORT
9117 Lake Shore Drive
Hague, NY 12836
[800]368-6088

JAMES NICKEL, ARCHITECT
PO Box 636
Victory Hill
Victory, VT 05858
[802]695-1071

PAT WOLFE
SCHOOL OF LOG BUILDING
RR #2
Lanark, ON K0G 1K0 Canada

DEL RADOMSKE'S
SCHOOL OF LOG BUILDING
1231 Phillpott Rd.
Kelowna, BC V1P 1J7 Canada

PUMPKIN MOUNTAIN GUN SHOP
Rt 28 & 30
Blue Mountain Lake, NY 12812
[518]352-7772